# Inspi*RA*tion for RAs

*Encouragement, Humor and Motivation for RAs by RAs*

**Amy Connolly**
**Tony D'Angelo**
**Dan Oltersdorf**

*The Collegiate EmPowerment Company, Inc.*

"The Leader in EmPowerment Education for Today's College Students"

D0074507

The Collegiate EmPowerment Company, Inc.
Lambertville, New Jersey
www.Collegiate-EmPowerment.com

Published by The Collegiate EmPowerment Company, Inc.
PO Box 702 - Lambertville, NJ 08530-0702
Toll Free: 1-887-338-8246
www.Collegiate-EmPowerment.com

Printed in the United States of America
ISBN: 0-9646957-1-5

*The
Collegiate
EmPowerment
Company, Inc.*

"The Leader in EmPowerment Education for Today's College Students"

# Table of Contents

**Acknowledgements/Dedication** ..................... 5

**Introduction** ...................................... 6

**Why Me?** ........................................... 7

Hopes of an RA ............................................. 8
What Were They Thinking? ................................... 9
Who Needs Fire Alarms? .................................... 11
An Eye for a...Laugh? ...................................... 13
The RA's Room ............................................. 16
Never Underestimate the Power of Potential ............... 18
Another Day ............................................... 19
What a Start .............................................. 21
Just Another Reason to Keep Your Door Locked ............. 22
A Pat on the Back ......................................... 24
Getting Your Feet Wet ..................................... 27
I Feel Like I Forgot Something... ......................... 29
It's Been a Long Night .................................... 30

**Tough Times & Conflict Resolution** .......... 36

The Night That Changed My Life ............................ 37
In the Strangest Places ................................... 38
Drawing the Line .......................................... 42
Never Judge a Book by its Cover ........................... 43
The one I didn't know ..................................... 45
The Tough Calls to Make ................................... 49
I Think I Can, I Think I can... ........................... 51
Take Time For Yourself .................................... 53
The ABCs for RAs .......................................... 56

**The Lighter Side** ................................. 58

The Perfect RA ............................................ 59
The Little Things ......................................... 60
Pretty in Pink ............................................ 63
Clearing the Air .......................................... 65
Mr. Pigg .................................................. 66
Lucky ..................................................... 67
Burning Down the House! ................................... 69
You'd Think They Would Learn! ............................. 71
Baptist Interviews ........................................ 75
Pager Go Down the Hole... ................................. 77

# Table of Contents

**Staff Support** ................................................. **78**

The Ties That Bind ........................................ 79
Muscular Dystrophy: A Positive Influence on Our Community ... 82
RA Unity .......................................................... 85
Making a Difference One Student at a Time ............... 87
Lifelines .......................................................... 90
My strengths, my coworkers, My FRIENDS ............... 93
Wear Your Staff Shirts ...................................... 95
Just Like Spice ................................................. 98
Behind Closed Doors.......................................... 99
Rebuilding Together .......................................... 102
It's When Things Seem Worse that You Must Not Quit. .......... 105
This is Who I Am.............................................. 109

**Acts of Kindness & Life Moments** ............. **112**

The Quilt ........................................................ 113
Memories Never Fade... .................................... 115
Christmas Surprise .......................................... 117
Reversed Roles ............................................... 118
My Best Program ............................................. 119
What Every College Creed Ought To Be ............... 120
Reaching Out .................................................. 121
The North Hall Boys ......................................... 125
Crisis by Candlelight ........................................ 130
A Kindness Revisited ....................................... 133
Moments to Remember...................................... 134

**About the Authors** ....................................... **139**
**More InspiRAtion!** ....................................... **140**
**Giving back to you** ....................................... **141**
**About ResidentAssistant.com** .................... **142**
**About The Collegiate Empowerment
Company, Inc.** ............................................... **143**
**Order Form**.................................................. **144**

# Acknowledgements and Dedication

This book is dedicated to all RAs, past and present, who serve on the front lines, giving their time, sacrificing sleep, shedding tears and building lifelong friendships with other staff members. You are the lifeline for your residents, and never forget that you have the power to make a difference!

**Amy** would like to thank her parents, Brian and Karen Connolly, for their never-ending love and support as well as her younger brother Tom and sister Sarah, for never ceasing to make her smile. In addition, she sends "cool beans" out to the entire student housing and dining staff at Northern Illinois University, especially Willard Draper, Blanche McHugh, Tim Trottier, Sarah Harlow, and Wendy Jo Peska for all of their guidance and encouragement. And lastly, Amy would like to thank her fellow R.As for the laughs, the tears, the long nights, the nights out, the karaoke, the movies, the pizza, the lessons, and of course, the love.

**Dan** would like to express his heartfelt thanks to the following: my family, who have done so much to bring me this far, the incredible housing staff at Colorado State University, for the fun times, the life lessons and all the wonderful experiences, my residents who have helped me to discover my passion for equipping and empowering students, as well as the countless individuals all over who have made ResidentAssistant.com a reality. I would also like to thank my wonderful wife Erin for all her love, friendship and never-ending support. Most importantly, I want to thank God, without whom I could do nothing.

**Tony** would like to thank the following for their unyielding love, support and strength: the team members of The Collegiate EmPowerment Company & EmPower X!, especially my personal assistant Pam Moss, the angels of Whizzer Bike Investments, our first client- the Department of Residence Life at Widener University who believed in us when others did not, my best friend and wife Christine and my creator-great spirit who guides me.

5

# Introduction

It started out simply enough. An R.A. from Northern Illinois University e-mailed an R.A. from Colorado State University about an idea – an idea that would bring R.A stories together from all over the country. Amy and Dan were so excited! So motivated! They put the word out on a website and a few discussion lists, and they set up an e-mail account. And then, they waited.

Enter Tony D'Angelo. With his many pep talks and several lessons about taking higher education deeper, Amy, Dan, and Tony formed the unstoppable team that would move on to compile this very book, *InspiRAtion for RAs.*

There is no one in the world that understands the day to day life of an R.A like another R.A. You know all about the unattended programs and the over crowded rooms. You know all about living in a glass box. You remember the long staff meetings. But you also remember the residents that make a difference in your lives everyday. You think about the memories from the staff retreat all the time. You love the late night pizza talks and the crazy movie nights. You've even come to love the tough nights on duty, because you know that you'll be stronger when you're through them.

This book is just the first step in what we hope will be a very long and fulfilling journey, and we'd like to invite you along for every step along the way. Take the stories you read within these pages and hold them close to your heart. Enjoy it. Love it. Live it.

*- Amy, Dan and Tony*

## One

# Why Me?

*Be like a postage stamp – stick to one thing until you get there.*
*-Josh Billings*

*Keep on going, chances are that you will stumble on something, perhaps when you are least expecting it. I never heard of anyone ever stumbling on something sitting down.*
*-Charles F. Kettering*

# Hopes of an RA

If you enter my room feeling lost
My hope is to show you direction.
If you enter my room full of tears
My hope is that you will leave with a smile.
If you enter my room feeling like a stranger
My hope is that when you leave,
We will know each other.
If you enter my room full of happiness
My hope is to share your excitement.
If you enter my room bothered by worry
My hope is that you will leave feeling at ease.
If you enter my room glowing with love
My hope is to share in your warmth.
If you enter my room bubbling with dreams
My hope is to watch them develop for you.
If you enter my room with a troubling problem
My hope is that you can confide in me.
If you enter my room
My hope is that we will both grow stronger.

Josh Feinblum
West Nottingham Academy - jfeinblum@wna.org

Submitted by:
Eric Marvin - RA - Hartford University
emarvin@MAIL.HARTFORD.EDU

*If you are interested in purchasing "Hopes of an RA" in
poster format, please contact:
The Collegiate EmPowerment Company
by calling toll free at 1-887-338-8246,
or email info@Collegiate-EmPowerment.com.

# What *Were* They Thinking?

It was a late cold winter night, and I was not on duty, but my friend Keith (name is changed to protect the bashful) was, and I wondered what was going on when he came running up to my top floor apartment. He was super excited about something. I figured he was dragging me out of my room to help bust some raging party, since it was the night before winter break began, and I was not looking forward to a confrontation. But it wasn't a party Keith wanted to show me.

About two weeks before, a decorative pine tree was chopped down in the back of our dorm, and public safety had put us on the alert to help find the choppers. Keith proceeded to show me a trail of pine needles that led from the outside door to the room across the hall, down the stairwell, and to the dumpster outside. And leaning right against the dumpster was the missing pine tree! Keith and I decided to play detective. We ran around in the freezing cold in just our pajamas trying to compare the stump in the back of the dorm to the stump on the tree- I was surprised that Keith didn't take DNA samples!

We finally decided to confront the room. I had let them borrow my vacuum cleaner earlier that day, so I just knocked on the door and asked for it back. Not only was their floor still covered with pine needles, but my vacuum cleaner (with the transparent dust compartment) was full of them too! I put my vacuum back in my apartment and got Keith to come with me to actually confront

them about the tree.  We had a trail of pine
needles leading up to their room, a pine tree out
by the dumpster, a vacuum cleaner full of pine
needles and a floor covered with tons of them as
evidence.  They of course tried to convince us that
it was a little wreath that someone's Mom gave
them, but needless to say, we weren't fooled!

Liane Letendre
Assumption College - lletendr@assumption.edu

*Oh, a trouble's a ton,*
*or a trouble's an ounce,*
*Or a trouble is what you make it,*
*And it isn't the fact that you're*
*hurt  that counts*
*But only how you take it.*
*-Edmund Vance Cooke*

*When the rock is hard, we get harder then the rock.*
*When the job is tough.  We get tougher than the job.*
*-George Cullum, Sr.*

# Who Needs Fire Alarms?

While serving as a Resident Assistant at the University of Illinois at Chicago, the Courtyard building's fire alarm was constantly going off. In one night the RA could respond to the system as many as three to four times! And as most of us know, alarms don't go off at a reasonable hour like 4 or 5 o'clock in the afternoon, it's more like 4 or 5 o'clock in the morning.

After a semester as an R.A, I was tired of responding to the fire alarm, of calling the desk to find out where it was activated, and going down the stairs to meet the fire department. I was tired of going to check the room and of finally going to reset the system.

One day the alarm went off - yet again. The time had come - enough was enough. I was going to quit this free room, board and stipend position and work at anything and anywhere besides this place. I returned to my room and I began to write my letter of resignation. I wasn't too far into it when there was a knock at my door.

Standing on the other side of the peephole was one of my residents, and she needed to talk. I invited her in and noticed at once that she seemed a little upset and emotional. I asked her if she needed anything to drink and she replied no. I asked her how her day was coming and she began to cry. I attempted to console her and let her know that if there was something I could help her with I would.

After I let her cry for a couple of minutes, she began to get her composure back and she began to speak. She told me that she was about to pack her bags and move out of the residence halls, she felt that she was no good at this thing called college. I allowed her to vent out all of her frustrations and disappointments, and after she finished, I asked her what her motivation had been when she applied and enrolled in college. She replied that she wanted to be a doctor so that she could help people, but that it seemed that she would not be able to help anyone because she could never understand what was going on in class. She continued to discuss the reasons for why she should quit and I listened. Then she asked me what she should do, and I told her that she should figure out how much she wanted to be a doctor.

Once she came to the conclusion that this was her true desire, she needed to fight for it. She needed to go to see the professor, find a tutor and study like she really wanted it. To become a doctor was going to mean a ton hard work and great grades. But that day, all that mattered was that she left my room with a smile on her face, ready to face the world. She completed the semester and continued with her passion to become a doctor.

After she left the room I looked over at my letter of resignation and tore it up. I came to the conclusion that no amount of fire alarms could keep me away from inspiring residents to be their best.

Danyale Ellis - Residence Hall Director
Western Kentucky University

## An Eye for a...Laugh?

It was my first year on staff. I was one of those people who came to the job certain that I could save the world by the virtue of my RA status. Unfortunately, after a month on staff, I was near the edge. I thought that I had to do everything, and that it had to be perfect. I was stressed out whenever I was off my floor and I was taking everything way too seriously. My supervisor along with my fellow staff members tried to put things in perspective, but I kept feeling like I wasn't doing enough perfect. As time went on, many factors combined to change my attitude, but one incident in particular changed my whole state of mind.

My staff and I had decided to hold a study abroad program. It was going to be very simple - we asked the director of off-campus study come to speak, and we drew a crowd by promising pizza. But being the slick Resident Coordinator that he was, my RC Marc decided not to order the pizza until after the program had begun so that we wouldn't be short or have too much.

Now picture it - we're all sitting there in the lobby listening to the speaker. I ribbed the other RAs because almost half of my residents had shown up. I myself decided to sit apart from the group, since I was hurrying to finish a gift that I was making for my mother's birthday. In all honestly, I wasn't really paying attention to where I sat, except to notice that there was a wooden box mounted on the wall near my head. The box is used at the end of the year for residents to return keys, so it wasn't something that I gave any extensive thought to. But I do remember making a mental note to be careful when I stood up.

Unfortunately, when my RC walked in carrying the pizzas, I jumped up to help him. Bad idea. The next thing I know, the speaker had stopped, everyone was looking at me, and my eye hurt beyond belief. I was so stunned I didn't scream or cry or anything. I immediately ran to the bathroom and it wasn't until on of my residents followed me into the bathroom and grimaced that I realized I was bleeding. Fortunately, I didn't injure my eye, but I was very lucky. I cleaned up my eye, put ice on it, and returned to the program to assure everyone that I was fine.

Later that night, I had another Res. Life meeting, and one of the other RAs who was a sports trainer, encouraged me to go to the Health Center. When they told me that I needed stitches, I wasn't thrilled. First of all, I am such a wimp and the mere thought thought of getting stitches near my eye was painful. Second, the last thing I wanted to do was to call my parents from the local emergency room and explain to them what had happened.

Luckily, they looked closer and saw that the wound wasn't large enough for stitches to do much good. It looked was like someone had stabbed me with a pen, two centimeters from my left eye. I still carry the scar. Every time I see it, I remember that I can never take myself too seriously and that life is too short and unpredictable to try to control every little thing. My fellow staff members still tease me, and I guess that's part of the lesson. So many things can go wrong and RAs, at least on college campuses, are the one who gets to deal with it all. Without a sense of humor, we'd never make it.

Kate Thompson
University of Texas
cathompson@mail.utexas.edu

*Fear less, hope more; eat less, chew more; whine less,*
*breathe more; talk less, say more; love more,*
*and all good things will be yours.*
*-Swedish proverb*

*Happiness is often the result of being*
*too busy to be miserable.*
*-Anonymous*

# The RA's Room

They walk down the hall on Move-In Day and see the open door with the "Resident Assistant" plaque. The room is empty because the RA is down the hall, busy checking someone in, inviting them to opening week activities, and soothing their nervous parents — who aren't entirely sure that they want to leave their child and go home.

There are posters on the wall. The corkboard holds pictures of smiling people — parents, siblings, and friends. The floor looks like a tornado has recently swept through. There are little bits and pieces of construction paper, bottles of glue and glitter, and tons of markers — does Picasso live here?? No, closer inspection shows that the remnants match the decorations that adorn Lisa's door, and Rebecca's and Amanda's.

The pillow on the bed looks like someone has recently taken a power nap...obviously lots of energy is needed when your day is spent meeting and greeting new faces. The planner on the desk has scribbles all over this week's open pages. Words like "duty" and "desk" and "orientation" and "training" seem to be demanding a lot of this R.As time. No wonder she needed a nap.

If they had a crystal ball, they'd be able to see into the future and view the many experiences and emotions that will take place within these four walls. They'd be able to see the R.A after a resident confrontation — although the residents thought she was having a "power trip," she was really just doing her job...it really wasn't the least bit enjoyable. They'd be

16

able to hear the fire alarm at 3 a.m. and see her reach groggily for her robe as she leaves her room to "dump" the building.

They'd be able to see how much it hurts when she plans a program that everyone wanted — but nobody attended. They'd be able to see the frustration she feels when she has a big test the next day, but keeps getting interrupted by well-meaning residents. It's not that they're trying to keep her from studying - they just need to tell her "one more thing."

They'd be able to see how good she feels when her residents plan an impromptu trip, and invite her along because "you're cool." They would see the joy that comes with a "You're doing an awesome job!" note from her RLD. They would see the relief she feels when her residents work together to deal with noise issues, and start to be less reliant on her to be the noise police.

They would see that the reason she spends so much time with her RA friends is *not* because the staff is excluding everyone else, but because they have a common bond that creates their support network.

As they walk toward their rooms, a woman with a handful of forms comes out into the hall. *Ah!! This must be the RA.* Talking with her, they decide she seems like a nice enough person, and as they think back to the glimpse they had of her room, they realize that — although she does represent the "authority", she's really just a person. A person who happens to be a student, a girlfriend, a sister, a daughter, and ...oh yeah, an RA.

Diedra Hader - Complex Director
Texas Tech University

# Never Underestimate the Power of Potential

In any given residence hall, at any given university, at any time during the school year, there lies within an abundance of potential. As RAs, we have the opportunity to see the potential played out in so many ways, both positive and negative. When you get discouraged, remember the power of potential, and the power you have to turn that powerful potential into positive results.

### *Don't underestimate your residents' potential...*

| | |
|---|---|
| ...to be brilliant | ...to point out your mistakes |
| ...to make poor decisions | ...to encourage you |
| ...to stretch you as a leader | ...to encourage each other |
| ...to help you to grow | ...to care |
| ...to make you happy | ...to be apathetic |
| ...to drive you crazy | ...to help you program |
| ...to give good advice | ...to never attend a program |
| ...to need good advice | ...to do well academically |
| ...to be amazing leaders | ...to need academic support |
| ...to make big messes | ...to develop and mature |
| ...to appreciate all you do | ...to be a community builder |
| ...to take you for granted | ...to make a negative impact |
| ...to love | ...to be a future RA |
| ...to repeat their mistakes | ...to be a future president |
| ...to learn from mistakes | ...to be your friend |

There is more potential in each one of your residents than you can imagine. Strive to help them achieve the positive and help them to transform the negative. Remember that you have the power to foster their positive potential by encouraging, confronting and caring for each and every one of your residents, no matter what type of "potential" they tend to display. Don't ever give up, and don't ever underestimate your power to help others achieve their potential!
Dan Oltersdorf
ResidentAssistant.com - dan@residentassistant.com

If you would like to order "Never Underestimate the Power of Potential" in poster format, call Toll Free: 1-877-328-8346 or email info@Collegiate-EmPowerment.com.

*Why Me?*

# Another Day

Each morning as I roll from bed
I wonder what will lie ahead
What will I face out there today?
Welcome to the life of an RA.

Tornado warnings, fire drills
Someone who took a chance with
sleeping pills
Broken glass and broken hearts,
Roommate friendships torn apart.

Another party down the hall
Another game of floor football
"Hey who began that water fight?"
"Who put in that porn on movie night?"

A six-page paper still to write,
Four different meetings, all tonight,
Another one where I'm up late,
Oh well I'll sleep after I graduate!

I often laugh, I sometimes cry,
I almost daily wonder "why?"
Why do I take on all this stuff?
An RAs job is just too tough!!

But when I think I've been stretched thin,
Someone asks, "Can I come in?"
"Thank you so much" they shyly say
"You really helped me out today."

# InspiRAtion for RAs

Then suddenly my mind is clear
And I remember why I'm here.
It's so much more than room and board,
My staff
My floor
The best rewards.


In my three years as a Resident Assistant, I have
had the opportunity to work with some of the best
residents that have ever passed through the halls
of my university. My staff has sustained me, and
I have never laughed so much as when I was
working as a resident assistant.

Amy Connolly – Resident Assistant
Northern Illinois University – tigger2@niu.edu


*If you are interested in purchasing "Another Day"
in poster format, please contact:
The Collegiate EmPowerment Company
by calling toll free at 1-887-338-8246,
or email info@Collegiate-EmPowerment.com.


*The world belongs to the energetic.*
*-Ralph Waldo Emerson*


*Do it big or stay in bed.*
*-Larry Kelly*

## What a Start

It was my first week as an RA. Classes had not yet started, and I was still feeling a bit jittery and nervous. I was going around and visiting all of the rooms on my floor to make sure that everyone was settling in all right, and taking care of some other business such as getting the residents' signatures and passing out some general information. I was finally beginning to feel more at ease.

I continued to work my way down the hall and in one room, I stopped to chat with one of the residents, when all of a sudden; I felt something tug at my pant leg! I looked down, and there was a little black Chihuahua. The resident saw the astonished look on my face and said, "So you didn't know about this either?" He said that he had just moved in, hadn't even met his roommate, but the dog had already peed on his bed, and under his desk. Needless to say I had a nice chat with the roommate later that day. What a way to start the year!

Jonathan Witenko – Resident Assistant
University of Florida – witenko@ufl.edu

# Just Another Reason to Keep Your Door Locked

This is a story that is a testament to good crisis management. When I was a Hall Director at a small private Catholic institution, we had a student who had come home one night three sheets to the wind. He was standing in his underwear banging on the Chaplain's door, wanting to talk to him, and making quite a ruckus. Now mind you, it's also 2:30 in the morning. So naturally, one of my RAs tried to reason with him, trying to make him stop kicking down the Chaplain's door. Finally, the RA and a few of his friends succeeded and the student went into a room. However, it was not his room.

This incident happened during Little Sibs weekend, and the true resident of the room (along with his 6-year-old brother) were inside the room that the drunk student went into. The true resident's roommate had not returned home yet. Now picture this in your mind: the older brother is sleeping in the top bunk, the little brother is sleeping in a sleeping bag on the floor, and in comes this very drunk and clumsy student. The drunk takes off his underwear, and completely naked, he lays down face first on the bed. To add insult to injury, he then urinates in the roommate's bed. My RA, who really did not want to mess with the drunken student, asked the two brothers to step out of the room and promptly called me.

## Why Me?

When I arrived on the scene moments later, I found the drunk student naked and passed out on the bed. He appeared to be cold and clammy so I immediately called security, who in turn called 911 (this is policy at this university). The medics came and put him on a soft stretcher and carried him down to the ambulance.

I know that at first, the story doesn't appear to be humorous. But the real kicker is that the drunken student's parents were on route from Buffalo, NY to visit him. And to top it off, he knew they were on their way when he went out to get bombed! When they got there at approximately six the next morning, they all met at the front stairs of the building. The parents were just getting here from a long drive; he was getting in from a long night in the hospital. I think that a long talk followed that.

Matthew Smith - Residence Life Coordinator
University of Akron - smith27@uakron.edu

*Optimism is essential to achievement and is also the foundation of courage and true progress.*
*-Nicholas Murray Butler*

# A Pat on the Back

Every once and a while, I would walk through the halls tired from my schoolwork, programs, staff meetings, and personal life, and I wondered if my efforts were really impacting my residents or simply remaining listless. My wing consisted of sixteen girls and I felt that I had a pretty good relationship with each of them. I also hoped to positively influence each of their lives in some way before the school year was over.

I had become a master at reading of their faces, the "I just failed a test" face, "My boyfriend is a jerk" face, "oops, slept through that class" face, "I miss home" face, "Why is life so hard and confusing" face and so on. But I had forgotten was that many of my girls had become skilled at reading my face just as well as I read theirs. On November 16, 1999, it became very apparent how well my residents really knew me, and I was reminded why I put forth my efforts in this job.

I remember having a long day at school; work not ever ending, some hard tests coming up, and boys were just about driving me crazy. It was a mixture of frustrations went on and on, and I didn't come back to the comforts of my dorm room until about ten that night.

With only one thing in mind, getting to my room ASAP, I walked quickly down the hall. On the way I was stopped by three of my girls who asked me if I was OK. I smiled and said, "I'm fine," and continued to scurry to my room. Approaching my door I fumbled with my keys, finally unlocked it, and quickly slammed the door be-

24

hind me, unaware that another resident had seen me in a hurry at the door and was going to approach me. After maybe five seconds, one of my girls pounded on my door. I opened it to see if she was OK, and she pushed her way in, commanded me to sit down, and told me I needed to let out whatever was on my mind. I was a little taken back. I felt like the roles had switched. Wasn't I supposed to be the one that helped them with their problems and not vice versa? I didn't say much at first, but and continued to stand her ground, saying, "Mel, I'm not leaving until you talk, you're human too." Although I still felt uncomfortable, I told her some of the basis of my frustrations. She gave me some encouragement, a hug, and said I knew where she lived. I thanked her and sent her on her way.

Finally, I felt a little better, and it was 11:00, and I was ALL by MYSELF. But five minutes after the first resident, another one knocked! I opened it and she said, "Hi, I know that when I'm mad I don't want to talk, so I just want to say hi and tell you that if you need me I'll be up for awhile. OK? Good night." I smiled, and thanked her too. I finally relaxed to some television, and fell asleep shortly after embracing the comforts of my bed.

The next morning I had the luxury of sleeping in, having only an afternoon class. I woke around noon, and I went to my closet to start my daily routine. As I went to leave for the showers, I saw that someone had slid a note under my door while I slept. It was a piece of printer paper with a hand drawn yellowish-orange rose in the middle with a quote besides it saying, "Life can be beautiful, but sometimes thorny." Around the edges of the paper, there was blue writing that encircled the page and looked like a frame to the beautiful flower. The message read:

"Melissa: I just wanted to send you a little rose to let you know that I was thinking of you. Believe me, I know that life is full of thorns and those thorns are hard to avoid. I am not going to begin to tell you however that I understand your pain. Instead, I wanted to let you know that you amaze me in so many ways. You are an ideal role model and friend in my life. Anyone who does not see all the beauty you possess is not worth your time. You are an extraordinary RA, sibling, daughter, and friend. You have accomplished so much at such an early age due to your ambition and intelligence. I love you and am thinking of you always."

This note immediately warmed my heart, brought some tears, and reiterated why I was an RA. I was here to impact people AND be impacted by others. Many RA's feel superior to their residents; I just feel grateful that I have this experience with them. They have taught me more than they will ever know, and their little "thank yous" touch my heart more than they could imagine. It is their small actions that I will take with me after this school year and feel confident that their lives were changed, even if for one moment, by me being their RA. All of the tests, programs, and meetings were worth it to get me to my position, and the girls are worth my efforts in staying in my position.

Melissa Kar – Resident Assistant
Arizona State University – mkar@arizona.edu

# Getting Your Feet Wet

Huh?! It kind of sounded like there was a knock at my door, and at seven in the morning, it probably wasn't just someone visiting. But then again, it was the first day of April, the day when nothing is what it seems and everything is a little out of whack, April Fool's Day.

I jumped out of bed and slowly opened my door. And there, leaning against my doorframe was a garbage can full of water. But thankfully, they had set me up wrong. I had heard of the prank before. You take a garbage can and fill it with water and then you set it against someone's door, knock and let the unfortunate victim open the door, splashing water into the room. But I guess they were amateurs, because when you set it against the doorframe instead of the actual door, that garbage can isn't going to move.

I looked down the hall and noticed that this wasn't just a prank designed for the RA, but for all the men on my co-ed floor. I went around the floor and took all of the cans down and emptied them out. And then, while I was on my little trek I heard some women in the bathroom talking. Now I know that eavesdropping is not a good thing, but I had already heard too much. Here were two of the women on my floor talking excitedly about how all the guys were going to get wet. Well, instead of grabbing the paperwork and filling out a report, I solved the problem the April Fool's way.

Before I emptied out the last can of water, I

propped it up against the women's bathroom door and proceeded to hop in the shower on the other end of the hall. Two minutes into the shower, I hear a scream. I got 'em!

That's the end of the story right? Nope, there's a final twist! I figured there would be no harm in putting the can against the bathroom door because there is a big drain on the floor where all the water would run into. The women would just get their feet and towels wet. Little did I know that the one drain on campus not working was on my floor in the women's bathroom! Oops! I guess the April Fool's joke was on me while we laughed as I told about my story and took care of the clean up.

Sean Anderson – Resident Assistant
University of Minnesota - anderssa@mrs.umn.edu

*We cherish our friends not for their ability to amuse us,*
*but for ours to amuse them.*
*-Evelyn Waugh*

## Why Me?

# I Feel Like I Forgot Something...

It was my second week as a first year RA in a building that is known around campus for it's numerous late-night fire alarms. Not just any fire alarms, *false* fire alarms. It was a fairly normal night. I went to bed after taking a walk around my floor to ask several people to quiet down. Once in bed, I fell asleep quickly, at least until about four o'clock in the morning - when I heard a loud noise outside my room. Groggily, I leapt out into the hall with the intention of scolding rowdy residents back into their rooms. But when I opened my door, lights and sirens overcame me.

Still sleepy, the one thought going through my head was, "Oh, I have to do something to get that turned off—Its quiet hours." Then I realized that the noise meant that I was supposed to do something, being an R.A and all. Without really thinking about it, I called the front desk, and highly agitated, asked, "What is that noise?" He politely responded with, "The fire alarm." Rats.

So I grabbed my jacket and shoes and began to help residents get out of the building. My first concern was for two students who couldn't hear the fire alarm on my floor. Another RA saw me trying to key into the room when he reminded me that it was January in Iowa, and said, "I'll key in. You should get some pants on." Oops. I had been so disoriented by the lights and sirens that I had simply forgotten! It was a night that I won't live down anytime too soon!

Author's Name Withheld by request

29

# It's Been a Long Night

It was the night from Hell
And I wasn't even on duty
The residents were loud
Of course!  It was ONLY 2:30!

Oh, the clinking of cans
I thought with chagrin,
Do these people realize
These doors are so thin?

I pounded on the door
"It's the CA!" I heard someone cry
I thought, "You guys woke me from sleeping,
I want someone to die!

I have class early tomorrow
And homework due, too!
It is WAY past quiet hours,
And that beer is taboo!"

They tried to look innocent
I asked for ID
"You WANT to cooperate.
Don't make me call the UP."

As I wrote the IR
My thoughts were so warm and sunny,
"I SO love to 'bust' people,
Cuz I do this job for the money!"

30

## Why Me?

This was a poem I wrote last year after one of "THOSE" nights. I thought it showed you need to keep your sense of humor to continue doing the job we do. I figured, instead of getting mad at someone, this was a good way to take out my frustration, and it gave people a few smiles and laughs after a long weekend, yes, at my expense, but if I could help, my poem served it's purpose.

Jenah D. Cousineau - Community Advisor
University of Wisconsin-Oshkosh
cousij45@mio.uwosh.edu

*When love and skill work together,*
*expect a masterpiece.*
*-John Rushkin*

*Try to forget yourself in the service of others. For when*
*we think too much of ourselves and our own interests, we*
*easily become despondent. But when we work*
*for others, our efforts return to bless us.*
*-Sidney Powell*

*Our greatest glory consists not in never falling, but in*
*rising every time we fall.*
*-Ralph Waldo Emerson*

*Education is hanging around until you've caught on.*
*-Robert Frost*

# Filling a Broom Closet With Love and Friends

The date was August 13, 1999. As a college sophomore, I was eager to move back to school. Not only was I looking forward to seeing all my friends after a summer at home, but I was eager to start training for my new job – as a Resident Assistant. I had been close to my RA the year before, and couldn't wait to become close with my own residents.

It seemed like thousands of programming ideas were in my head. My best friend Eric (who was an RA at another local college) and I had spent some time coming up with door tag ideas. I was more than willing to cut my summer short a week early to start training. Even though it was 90 degrees outside, I was looking forward to a week of learning with new and old R.As.

I called school ahead of time to get room dimensions for a rug. After being told my room was 12x15, I bought a 9x12 rug. We drove two hours to school. I met my Resident Director and got the key to my room. My cousin and I lugged the rug up to my new room. I opened the door and just stared.

Was this really a room? Had this been a broom closet at some previous time? Was I really expected to live in this hole in the wall? To put the size of my room in perspective, we laid down the 9x12 rug. It didn't fit in the room. How was I supposed to fit a bed, wardrobe closet, desk, dresser, refrigerator, and television in here, along with all of my personal belongings? Weren't R.As supposed to have room for residents to come in and sit? I certainly didn't!

The whole situation was made even worse by the condition of the dorm itself. It had been renovated over the summer and wouldn't be complete for another week. There were no shower curtains. Of course, that didn't make a difference because we had to walk to the nearest dorm for showers anyway - we had no hot water at all. Everything was filthy from dust and dirt and at all hours of the day and night, maintenance workers were using loud machinery, trying to get the dorm ready in time for residents. The phones weren't working. Cable came and went sporadically. And last but not least, rumors are always flying that our dorm is haunted, so I was probably sharing my small hole in the wall with one or two ghosts.

Was I crazy? What had I gotten myself into? I thought being a RA was going to be so much fun. Could I be wrong? Could I stand living like this? The situation seemed horrible. I begged for a new room. I begged on behalf of the other three RAs above and below me with the same size room. I begged until I was blue in the face. I was eventually given the choice of moving into a new room ... not as a RA but as a resident.

I thought about it for a long time. The walls of my room seemed to move in a little closer the longer I thought. During this time, a housekeeper brought me a vacuum to keep in my room.

I was convinced I would have to move out because there wasn't room for the both of us!

At this point, I left my room and started talking with returning R.As about the job. I really wanted to be a RA. I had been looking forward to it since I received the acceptance letter last March. I couldn't just throw out all my programming ideas! But I couldn't live in the broom closet either. I was really stuck and couldn't decide what to do. Eventually, I ended up at the door of – who else – my former RA. She seemed to know everything last year, so she would certainly know what to do this time.

Once my phone was working, I called Jenn and talked to her. She came over and helped me rearrange my room so that it was livable. Then she talked with me and gave me advice. She asked me why I took the job, since she knew that I didn't take it for the money. I simply wanted to do for others what my RA had done for me. I realized that I was doing this job to help people, not to get a luxurious room.

I ended up staying in residence life as a RA. I couldn't be happier that I made that decision. I've managed to move my room around so that I have more than enough space to live in. Sure, it's not ideal, but I do just fine. I've received numerous awards, and it's the little things that have made the difference. A resident baking me cookies for Christmas was a great reward. Little thank you notes from residents on my door made the situation great. Late night talks with residents who have come to trust me as a friend have made the job perfect. Having residents come see a musical production just because I am in it have made this worthwhile. Perhaps the most rewarding part was having residents apply to be Resident Assistants next year because they wanted to do for others what I did for them.

These things have made the job worthwhile, not the size of my room. I wouldn't have given up this experience for my own apartment on campus. My residents have helped me just as much as I've helped them. And the greatest reward of all has happened: I've become that Resident Assistant that I looked up to last year. I have had such an influence on other people that they want to do the same. I've made a difference on campus, and I did it all from my broom closet that I've turned into a home. Any RA's room can be that way. It's not the size of the room, but the size of the heart of the RA, that makes even a broom closet a perfect home.

Cristin M. Chase - Resident Assistant
St. Bonaventure University - chasecm@yahoo.com

*All that is necessary is to accept the unacceptable, do without the indispensable, and bear the unbearable.*
*-Kathleen Norris*

*Whenever you fall, pick something up.*
*-Oswald Avery*

# Two

# Tough Times & Conflict Resolution

*Faith in oneself…is the best and safest course.*
*-Michaelangelo*

*In the darkest hour the soul is replenished and given strength to continue and endure.*
*-Heart Warrior Chosa*

*The crisis of today is the joke of tomorrow.*
*-H.G. Wells*

# The Night That Changed My Life

It was the summer break and I was staying on campus, working as a RA on a co-ed floor. My floor had never given me any real problems until that one fateful night. It was a weeknight and a young woman was on our floor visiting one of my residents. Later that night that same young lady was found naked in my floor lounge. Right from the start it appeared that she had been raped.

It took a few days to sort out all of the information but eventually it was confirmed – we were dealing with a gang rape situation. The reports ran that anywhere from 5 to 10 people were involved - all of who lived on the floor. Those who weren't involved were scared out of their minds. In all honesty, so was I. I didn't know what to do. I felt responsible. I know now that there wasn't anything I could do but still, at the time I felt like I had let this girl down.

While I was dealing with this I had the support of most of my staff; they were all as shocked as I was, and I also had friends that helped me out. I knew that this experience could only make me stronger as a person and an R.A. I still think about her, and I wonder if I did all I could, but now I know that I can face any challenge that life throws at me. This job has given me confidence that I never knew I had and that's why I have stayed in it for three years. No matter what happens in life I know I will always be prepared.

Jen Crompton – Resident Assistant
Northern Illinois University – jcrompto@niu.edu

# In the Strangest Places

As RA's and residential staff members, we are all trained to deal with scary situations and crises that we hope we'll never actually have to confront. Often we have to face incidents that involve people we don't know very well, or have known for only a short time and those, I think, are very difficult. However, I was at a staff meeting recently where the topic of the development discussion was suicide.

My bout with a suicide incident was unusual in two respects: first, it was a student who didn't even attend my University, and second, this student lived a hundred miles away. Her name is Jen, and she was my best friend in high school. She went to Penn State and started dating a boy, who was planning on transferring to my tiny little school in Virginia. The fall he was to begin attending my school, Jen decided to take some time off to make some decisions about her life.

Jen came to visit me one weekend in September. It was a little strange because her boyfriend lived in my building as well, so Jen was able to spend time with both of us. She also became friends with all of my friends from school. I remember thinking that it was awesome that all of my friends got along so well. And then I found out after she had left for home, Jen and her boyfriend had broken up while she was here. I made the assumption that if she wanted to talk to me about it she would e-mail or call. We had always had a very open and honest friendship in that respect.

## Tough Times and Conflict Resolution

I remember the day very clearly. It was a Wednesday and it was starting to get brisk. I went to choir at about one o'clock. About fifteen minutes into my rehearsal, my roommate interrupted the class to find me. She said that Jen had left a message on the voice mail and I needed to call her immediately to make sure she was all right. I didn't comprehend what my roommate was telling me, but I suddenly I was running across campus to get to my room.

I listened to the message Jen left so that she could basically say "goodbye." She was thanking me for being her best friend. I was numb. I remembered hearing tons of stories in RA training about scenarios that I would have to face with my residents, but I never dreamed I'd have to deal with one concerning my best friend.

I called back and got her on the phone as quickly as I could. My heart was racing a million miles an hour, but I continued to talk to her as if we were just chatting. Meanwhile, my friends had followed me into my room, having guessed what was happening from bits and pieces my roommate had been able to tell them. I had to communicate with the people in the room with a pad of paper, because I had made a deal with Jen promising that I wasn't going to tell anyone else what was going on. On that pad of paper, I wrote instructions to get one of the other RA's and to go to another room to call my supervisor. I desperately needed back up and support.

Jen and I sat a hundred miles apart and talked for two hours. I felt so helpless, and my first instinct was to get into my car and drive home. However, I realized that option would give her two hours by herself, and I couldn't leave her alone for that long.

I was able to get her to tell me about what she was feeling and what her plans were. I felt so scared. This was my best friend telling me that there was nothing worth living for. We had been through everything, and she felt that she had found something that we couldn't handle. I found out what medications she was taking, or not taking, as the case turned out. She had stopped taking her Prozac, because she didn't want to anymore. We talked about that for a while, and then we talked about her breakup with her boyfriend. I think that was the main reason behind her desire to die. It scared me. For college students, breaking up with a significant other is an everyday event, and I work with 45 freshmen women. Who knew what was going on in my hallway?

While I kept Jen on the line and tried to stay calm, my residence life director sat beside me and coached me through my pad of paper. One of my fellow RA's sat out in the hallway with a portable phone and somehow got in contact with the police in my little hometown. She was able to give them directions to Jen's house, so that someone could go be with her.

When police officer arrived at Jen's house, I held my breath as she answered the doorbell and spoke with him. She promptly came back to the phone and yelled at me. But in all honesty I didn't care. Then the officer spoke with me to find out what had been going on, and to let me know that she would be safe. I said goodbye, and hung up the telephone.

I turned to face my room, and realized that there were ten people sitting and standing in my little cube. As soon as I set the phone down, just about all of them came over and gave me a giant hug. I was totally overwhelmed by the support of my friends and staff members, and also with my courage and strength.

I now knew that if I could save my best friend a hundred miles away, I could do a lot for the people who live ten feet away. I knew that I had made an important difference in the life of a young woman who was dealing with ordinary everyday issues, and it made me a stronger person, friend, and RA.

Kate Gibson – Resident Assistant
Shenandoah University - kgibson@su.edu


*One thing at a time, all things in succession.*
*That which grows slowly endures.*
*-J.G. Hubbard*

# Drawing the Line

Being an RA in a house where most of the people I supervised were the same year as me was very hard my first year. It was tough starting out and thinking that I might have to crack down on my friends. But to make it easier, I did it from day one. I sat everyone down, told them how excited I was about the year and how we would be the coolest house on the campus. And then came the hard part. I told them that I still had a job to do and that I would operate the house under one ideology, RESPECT. What was done behind closed doors was your own business unless you made it the business of others. They all looked at me and said, "No problem."

But just a week later, I had to confront an underage drinker who was drinking in the hall. Needless to say, he was not very happy but he came to me the next day to apologize. He said that he had jeopardized our friendship and placed me in a very awkward position. He vowed to never do it again and told everyone else in the house that he was wrong.

From that day on, I never had a problem and I ended up with the coolest house on campus. It was so cool - once the seniors had chosen to move into the senior dorm the following year, our house was the first to be filled up by upperclass students. It's amazing what a little respect and honesty can accomplish.

By Kirby Palkoner, submitted by Laura Palkoner, Northern Illinois U- pooh_niu@hotmail.com

# Never Judge a Book by its Cover

When you step into the resident assistant role, your life changes. Whether the change is good or bad is strictly a question of perception. Originally I took the position for many selfish reasons: the money, room and board, and notoriety. There were obligations that I knew about beforehand such as on-calls, front desk hours, bulletin boards, and programs, but two unseen concepts surprised me when I settled into the position.

The first unrecognized topic was my time. Knowing that the job would take a lot of free time away from me, I thought that I was going to have to try really hard to juggle my job, my schoolwork, and my responsibilities to the other organizations that I belonged to. For example, my second semester as an RA, I took a C++ computer programming class. The class wasn't unusually hard, but if one didn't put enough time into it, it would become very difficult to do well in. Due to planning my schedule late, I ended up with many weekend on-calls, requiring me to be in my building a lot. So instead of spending my Friday and Saturday nights drinking or partying with other classmates, I spent time reading and programming. But as a direct result of the free time that was supposedly taken away from me, I was circumstantially drawn into studying more and I achieved a solid 'A' in my class.

The second unusual revelation dealt with my major—engineering. Although I realized that working as an RA looked good on a resume, I did not think the skills would ever apply to my major. "How can doing bulletin boards, weekly reports, and programming ever help me become a better engineer?" was the big question I had in the back of my mind. I even considered not returning to the RA position the next year since I didn't think the "skills" were an advantage. But then I had the opportunity to take some time off from school to do a cooperative (co-op). For engineering students this is similar to a six month internship or a small "real-world" job. And everyday in my new job I experienced something in the "real-world" that had significance and the co-op made me realize what kinds of skills would be needed if I wanted to be a successful engineer. To my surprise, everyday I used skills that the RA position either instilled or enhanced in me. Skills like brainstorming, planning, organizing, preparing, facilitating, and following up are great examples of how the RA position and the engineering job are closely related. The other observation I discovered was that engineering and management are tied very closely together as well.

As a result, when I came back to school, I added a business administration minor and within the residence halls I applied for the program director position, which uses more managing skills. My newfound enthusiasm and experience landed me the PD position where I am thankful everyday I have this great job.

Adam Draeger – Resident Assistant
University of Wisconsin at Platteville
draeger@uwplatt.edu

# The one I didn't know

The one resident that I didn't know could have been the only one I didn't forget.

I was a first year RA at Millikin University. My floor consisted of mostly first year women who were all slowly turning 19 years old. At 19, students can go over to Champaign-Urbana and get into bars, so this birthday is usually a pretty big deal.

I didn't know it was Beth's 19th birthday.

I spent that Friday night in Champaign Urbana with my best friend, one of my few non-staff friends. We went from coffeehouse to coffeehouse, trying to stay warm. It was a frigid Midwest night, but the skies were clear.

I didn't know that Beth was engaged.

I got back to my floor and slipped into bed. I was looking forward to sleeping through the duty free night peacefully and catching up on well-needed rest.

I didn't know that Beth's fiancé had joined the Army.

The sound of residents pounding on my door woke me up. "Leah! Leah! Beth can't breath. She's not breathing! Leah! WAKE UP!" I got my

45

sweatpants on and raced down the hall to Beth and Jennifer's room. Five of us in one room and one was unconscious. I had never seen anybody before in as bad of shape. She wasn't breathing, her hands were clenched and she was having seizures.

I didn't know that Beth's fiancé had left for boot camp on her 19th birthday.

I called the hall director on duty and told the girls to go and get her from downstairs. I raced to the ground floor to the Public Safety office to request an escort to the hospital. The officer met the women in the stairwell and yelled for the dispatcher to call 911. She needed an ambulance, a call I didn't know to make. We laid Beth on the couch and I sent each resident to a different door to wait for paramedics. Jennifer, Beth's roommate waited in the lounge with the security officer and the HD. I paced the hallway checking doorways and talking to Liz and Ruth. I explained the best I could what was happening.

I didn't know that Liz and Ruth would soon be RA's themselves.

It was late enough that nobody wandered through the lounge that had been converted into an emergency room. As fire trucks, ambulances, and paramedics arrived, I stood back and watched them try to bring Beth back to life. The energy was high, but my residents were as calm as could be expected.

I didn't know that Beth had celebrated with Mad Dog and aspirin.

Nobody cried that night, not yet.
I didn't know that Beth would drop out.

It was adrenaline that finally stabilized Beth. They put her on a stretcher and took her to the hospital. My lounge was now a lounge again. I sent Liz and Ruth back to bed with promises of news in the morning. Jennifer and I went to the HD's car and followed to the true ER, where Beth was being treated.

I didn't know that Beth got married.

While we tried to get all the information from her emergency information card entered into the computer system, we didn't know what was happening behind the doors. It didn't take long to get the news.

I didn't know that she would have a baby by her next birthday.

And the news didn't come from a doctor, but from Beth as she walked out of the back. She was angry and didn't know why she was there. We tried to convince her to stay, to find out what had happened. She refused treatment and we never got answers.

I was the only person who knew the snow

started at 7:13 AM.

That night, I stayed up until the snow started to fall. I had my radio on. My television on. My computer on. My lights on. And my door was open when I finally fell asleep. I wanted my women to know that it was never wrong to wake me up. And if anything else happened I wanted to be ready.

I still know every minute of that night.

Beth came up to me that afternoon and gave me a red sweater. She had been given it in the ER, because she hadn't taken a jacket. Her roommate returned the jacket to the security officer. I still have the red sweater.

I never knew what to do with it.

Beth eventually left school, got married and started her family. Her roommate lost touch with her after the wedding. Jennifer went on to study abroad and have a successful time at Millikin. Liz and Ruth, the next-door neighbors, became RA's. I have since sent more residents to the hospital after suicide attempts. Now I am an RD and when the ER was in a different lounge at a different school, I thought about Beth.

And that was the night that I cried.

Leah Jones - Residence Director of Cooper Hall
Fort Lewis College - jones_l@FORTLEWIS.EDU

# The Tough Calls to Make

It was my first semester as a Graduate Resident Director. We had already completed our summer training session both for RDs and R.As and I had done my best to inspire and motivate my staff. I learned from them and they learned from me. It was really exciting to see them form into a cohesive team, each supporting the other in programs, training and of course, "on-the-job situations." Even more so, they were friends. There was that special sense of trust, commitment and respect that is crucial for any group or organization to have in order to effectively accomplish its goals.

And then came the news from the RD on duty one fateful night: "I saw one of your R.As on duty, having a beer at the bar." I could feel my palms start to sweat and my heart began to race. I knew from the strict policy regarding staff drinking while on duty that I would be losing one of my staff members.

There I was, faced with a policy on the one hand and on the other, the fact that I had worked so hard to build a team and that this person was an integral part of that team. Indeed, the RA was a productive member on my staff. More so, this individual possessed such intangibles as sincerity, generosity and creativity that are critical to being an RA.

The next morning, I met with the RA and my supervisor. Tearfully, the RA admitted to having a "sip of beer." The RD on duty noted that the RA was not visibly intoxicated. In essence, the situation boiled down to a good RA who had made a bad decision and the policy issue. It was then that I began to question the nature of what we do as a whole in Residence Life. Can exceptions be made to a policy? Under what conditions do we draw the line in the sand? What is the best course of action for the organization in congruence with its stated mission? What would the impact be on the other staff members if the RA was fired or if the R.A stayed on? How would resident students react to whatever course of action was pursued? And from a personal standpoint, how would I be viewed if I "went to bat for this person?" Armed with these questions, I proceeded in dialogue with my colleagues and supervisors.

Ultimately, there were other factors that came into play that impacted the final decision. However, the lesson to be learned is that it is only through the thoughtful engagement of questioning and dialogue that we are forced to realize our fullest potential in Residence Life. I believe the culture of Residence Life is one that allows us the freedom to continually question what it is we do and how we can do it better. It is this culture that inspires me to say not "Why, me?" but "Thankfully, me!"

Dana E. Jarvis - Graduate Resident Director
University of Pittsburgh - djarv4@yahoo.com

# I Think I Can, I Think I can...

It was my first year as an RA, and despite the fact that I had been through all of the incredibly extensive training that my university could throw at me I was still feeling very nervous. I just kept thinking, what if I actually had to confront someone? It was my biggest fear. We had practiced by confronting people in training, but that was different, it was all just role-playing. And on my first night of duty, slowly but surly ten o'clock rolled around and it was time for me to do my first set of rounds.

Luckily, another RA who was also a good friend of mine was willing to accompany me. We checked for love birds in the sauna and T.V. lounge, looked out for people attempting to throw computers out of the window in the lab, and of course, kept an eye out for those residents that were unwinding with a few too many bottles of alcohol before the first day of classes.

We live in a small residence hall with only four floors and eight wings. The first floor was quiet, and the same on the second. Third floor was quiet...and then we smelled it - Yes that's right, the stairwell leading up to the fourth floor smelled like Bo's (a local bar) at last call.

Suddenly, my heart began to race - it was actually happening, the first incident of the year! Bravely, we walked up the stairwell and took a quick sweep of the floor. To my right, a mop closet was being cleverly disguised as a bathroom by the young gentleman relieving himself in the mop closet sink. We continued to walk on, encountering two gentlemen too drunk to remember how to work a doorknob, who proceeded to introduce themselves. Obviously they were unaware that we were RAs (that is the best when they don't know who all the RAs are yet!).

When we reached the offending room, we put our training to the test and called our beloved security (every RA's angels and headaches). While we were waiting for their arrival, we hung out by the door of the room collecting the IDs of anyone that left. When security came, breathalyzer tests were given, citations were written, and the beer bottles and cans were collected, counted, and dumped. And then it was over, just like that.

Going through my first incident was scary and the butterflies in my stomach escaped only while finishing up the paperwork that night. The confrontations I had dreaded throughout RA training lost their potency on my nerves. This incident may sound like a minuscule thing to most people, but for me it was a turning point. I realized how strong I was and that although I didn't think training prepared me to be a good RA, I was. I found something in myself that night that I didn't think I had, confidence. I am having a wonderful year, I love my job as an RA, and plan on coming back next year!

Laura Hanson – Resident Assistant
University of Wisconsin @ River Falls
laura.a.hanson@uwrf.edu

# Take Time For Yourself

I was a first-year resident assistant on an all-male floor. I started at the beginning of February, and came into a community where all of the residents had LOVED their previous RA. There was one new resident on the floor and I spent a lot of time trying to help him adjust to life at college. This resident, I'll call him Brad, seemed to be getting along fine with all the rest of the people on the floor. He was good-looking, athletic, and just an all-around good guy to talk with.

Since I became an RA so late into the semester, I was receiving my training slowly from my direct supervisor over time. One night after I went to sleep another RA knocked on my door and keyed in at the same time. Of course I woke up and asked what was the matter. Since I did not hear any noise (a first for my floor) I had no idea what could be so urgent. She was in a hurry, grabbed my sub master (the key that opened all the rooms on my floor) and said something about one of my residents trying to jump out his 10th story window.

I was fully awake and out of bed instantly. Here I was, first few weeks of my job, trying to make a good impression and provide leadership to a bunch of younger guys, and all I could do was stand in the hallway helpless as the police and the senior staff tried to talk this resident (who I thought I knew all about) into opening his door. Finally they convinced him to open the door and wrestled him to the ground as he made a running start for the window.

I had a hard time going back to sleep that
night. The next morning, I was still shaken. To
be honest, I felt like I had failed as an RA. I received a phone call from the front desk telling me
that Brad's mom was downstairs and that she
needed to get into his room. I remember it was
really hard to see her – I just didn't know what to
say. I let her in to get a few of Brad's things. She
told me he would be returning to the floor in a
couple of days. I did my best to keep Brad's confidence, even though some residents wanted to
know why the police had been there, and where
Brad was. It wasn't easy.

What really stands out in my memory was a
follow-up meeting with my supervisor the day
after the incident. He debriefed me about all the
procedures in motion, asked if I had any questions, and reminded me about guarding Brad's
confidentiality with the other residents. And then
he said something I don't know if I will ever forget.
My supervisor asked "But how are YOU doing?"

We went on to have a long discussion about
how I felt about everything that happened and he
helped me process through the entire incident.
When I left his office that afternoon, I knew what
it meant when someone said, "staff support." My
other RAs in the tower were also great, but it was
what my supervisor Jim said that really helped
me get through the incident and grow from it.

After some recuperation time, Brad did indeed
come back to finish the rest of the semester. The
following year he moved out of the halls and into a
fraternity. The last time I saw him he remem-

bered me.  We talked a little.  He was president of his fraternity, getting ready to graduate that May, and move on with his life.  I remember he seemed so happy.

I was so thrilled to see how well he had over-come the obstacles in his life with some help from dedicated and caring people. My supervisor helped me see that I was one of those people who COULD make a difference in someone else's life. I was just glad to be there to do what I could, even if that meant I just did my job.

James E. Mitchell – Graduate Assistant for Programming Resoureces
Northern Illinois University
resource_center01@yahoo.com

*Yesterday I dared to struggle.  Today I dare to win.*
*-Bernadette Devlin*

## The ABCs for RAs

**A** - Ask for help! You aren't alone, and you probably aren't the expert. Utilize the resources on your staff, in your hall and on your campus. Think of yourself as an "Referral Agent." Know when to refer and who to refer to!

**B** - Balance is very important. Remember you are a student first, then an RA. Prioritize the various commitments you have andcontinually self evaluate to find out if you are out of balance. If you find yourself unbalanced, talk to someone about it!

**C** - Consistency is key! If you aren't consistent, it will come back to haunt you. Treat everyone fairly and don't let anything "slide."

**D** - Don't take things personally. When residents violate policy, it is not usually directed at you as a person!

**E** - Evaluate and assess the needs of your residents. At the beginning of the year, and on an ongoing basis, do formal and informal assessments to find out what your residents need!

**F** - Fun should always be part of the job! If you aren't having fun, you need to take a step back and look at what you are doing. If all you do is policy enforcement, you are missing out!

**G** - Get to know your residents, and be sure to remember their names. Make picture flashcards if you have to!

**H** - Have a servant's attitude, but don't let yourself be tread on or taken advantage of.

**I** - Invest your time with care because it is a valuable commodity. Use a day timer. Don't over-commit, and remember how to say the magic word, "no."

**J** - Just be yourself! Let your residents see you as a person, not just an RA.

**K** - Know that you can't please everybody.

L - Laugh when things get crazy! Sometimes it's all you can do to stay sane.

**M** - Maintain a solid front with your staff. If residents are "dissing" another staff member, don't join in, even if you agree with them!

**N** - Never share confidential information you know about a resident! If you respect your residents, they will respect you.

**O** - Open your door, but know when to lock yourself in for some "me-time."

**P** - Program, program, program! Plan programs and activities that help your residents to grow, socially, academically and personally!

**Q** - Quality time with residents is better than a large quantity of programs. Programs are essential, but be sure to just "hang out" with your residents too.

**R** - Remember why you became an RA. Write down what your reasons are for being an RA, and put them in a place you can refer to on a regular basis.

**S** - Study! In addition to the fact that academics come first, you are a role model for your residents.

**T** - Take care of yourself. If you don't take care of yourself, how will you be able to take care of your residents?

**U** - Understand the variety of developmental levels your residents are at, as well as the various backgrounds they have come from, and the variety of views and beliefs they hold. Seeking to understand them more completely will help you relate with them and serve them better.

**V** - Value this great opportunity to help others!

**W** - Working as a team with your fellow staff is a key to success.

**X** - Examine your own values, beliefs and background, so you know your own biases. This understanding of self will help you to better understand others, which is very important for working with a diverse group of people.

**Y** - You have on of the most important jobs on campus!

**Z** - Z's! – Get some rest!

Dan Oltersdorf
ResidentAssistant.com
dan@residentassistant.com

*If you are interested in purchasing "The ABCs for RAs"
in poster format, please contact:
The Collegiate EmPowerment Company
by calling toll free at 1-887-338-8246,
or email info@Collegiate-EmPowerment.com.

# Three

# The Lighter Side

*You grow up the day you have your first real laugh at yourself.*
*-Ethel Barrymore*

*Circumstances – what are circumstances?*
*I make circumstances.*
*-Napoleon Bonaparte*

*Keep breathing.*
*-Sophie Tucker*

# The Perfect RA

1. Bob Smith, Resident Assistant, can always be found
2. hard at work on his floor. Bob works proactively, without
3. lying to his Hall Directors or drinking with residents.  Bob never
4. thinks twice about helping his fellow RAs, and he always
5. finishes his assignments on times.  Often he takes extended
6. measures to complete his work, sometimes skipping
7. vacations.  Bob is a Resident Assistant who has absolutely no
8. vanity in spite of his time, accomplishments and profound
9. knowledge in his field.  I firmly believe that Bob can be
10. classified as a high-caliber RA, the type which can not be
11. dispensed with.  Consequently, I duly recommend that Bob be
12. named Resident Assistant of the Year, and a proposal will be
13. executed as soon as possible.

Addendum:
That idiot was standing over my shoulder while I
wrote the report sent to you earlier today.
Kindly reread only the odd numbered lines.

Meghan Dorn – Resident Assistant
Arizona State University - megsadevil@yahoo.com

*The most important single influence in the life of a
person is another person...
-Paul D. Shafer*

# The Little Things

I had been having a lot of heart to heart talks with one of my residents and we were becoming very close. One night she said to me, "One of my friends has been having a hard time lately and he e-mailed me and told me that he wished that there was a magic switch that he could turn on when he felt sad that would help to make him happy and feel better about himself." She looked right at me and continued, "I wrote him and I told him that you were my magic switch." It was the sweetest thing!

**********************************************************

A few weeks ago, I was having a pretty rough day and I was feeling very stressed out. I had been really busy and overwhelmed with my own studies and my floor. I came back from class only to find a sign rolled up on my pillow. I opened it up and it was a big, yellow sunshine and it read,

*"You are my RA, my special RA,*
*You make me happy when times are bad.*
*I want you to know Jess, I'm glad I found you.*
*Just like Mr. Right will find you someday."*

It was supposed to be sung to the tune of "You are my Sunshine." Needless to say, my day was a lot brighter because of that.

These are just a few of the times that my residents have inspired me or made me smile when I felt down.

Jessica Nye - Resident Assistant
Central Michigan Univ – nye1jn@mail.cmich.edu

# Fun With Paperwork

09.30.99

At approximately 00:05 zulu hours Bean West duty RA's Hollee Thetford and Gabe Silverman observed a gentlemen exiting Ganoe room #450. Upon establish-ing visual contact with Thetford, the suspect re- entered the room and closed the door.

Remembering their Navy Seal training, Silverman and Thetford observed #424 and heard clinking bottles and loud talking coming from the room. At approximately 00:07 zulu hours Thetford and Silverman terminated radio silence and identified themselves as Air Force Paratroopers and re-quested visual contact with the suspects. After hearing rustling and waiting nearly 40 seconds, the door was opened partially by a young woman who later identified herself as Michelle Lastname1, one of the room owners.

After requesting the door be opened completely, Lastname1 complied and Thetford observed a can of Budweiser beer in the room. Silverman and Thetford explained their suspicion, discussed the blatant disregard for the community under con-struction, and asked if anyone else was in the room. Sean Lastname2 and Erin Lastname3, (room-mate of Lastname1) emerged from the right side of the room, not visible from Silverman and Thetford's position at #450's companionway. Thetford and Silverman explained that the situation they observed would be documented. All residents were cooperative and non- confrontational. The occupants willingly produced 2 bottles of alcohol which they disposed of at Silverman and Thetford's request and admitted that a water bottle also contained alcohol and agreed to empty it's contents as well.

Silverman and Thetford advised the occupants of the room that the alcohol containers would need to be disposed of promptly and advised floor RA Denise Salmonson of the situation. This situation yielded no MIA's, WIW's, POW's, or COW's.

Civilian casualty rate: 0% Accuracy ratio: 70% GPA: Top Secret.

**Mark (our Resident Director / Direct Supervisor), I think that our lack of night vision goggles in this particular situation hampered our ability to effectively construct community.

*Room number has been changed

Gabe Silverman – Resident Assistant
Oregon State University -
Gabe@GeckoDesigns.com

> *If you want to do something, do it!*
> *-Plautus*

> *Even if you're on the right track, you'll*
> *get run over if you just sit there.*
> *-Will Rogers*

# Pretty in Pink

During my first semester as an RA, I was assigned to the staff social committee. As the holidays approached, one of the ideas that I developed was a Christmas party. Part of the idea for the Christmas party was to have a Secret Santa activity where everyone would draw names, and then buy something for the person whose name they had drawn. I felt that the party could be one of the highlights of the semester, and a great way to leave for break.

After finding a restaurant to host the party, I started on the Secret Santa project. I set up some guidelines for the activity. Each staff member was expected to give gifts or do good deeds at least 5 times during exam week with a final gift exchange at the Christmas Party to be held the last night of exams.

To help everyone with gift ideas, I compiled a list of personal preferences for each staff member by sending out an e-mail with six standard questions. I asked the staff to each respond with their answers. I made a table on my word processing program and kept it easily accessible on my computer's desktop so that I could input everyone's responses as they came in. About one week before the Secret Santa activity was supposed to begin, I sent out the completed chart over e-mail as an attachment entitled simply "Staff Wish List."

Shortly after I sent out the e-mail, a fellow staff member called me in my boyfriend's room to ask me if I was certain I had sent out the correct at-tachment. I replied, "I think so. Why?" She replied, "Maybe you should check it out." So, I looked at the e-mail on my boyfriend's computer and opened the attachment. It contained only a few items, including "Victoria's Secret Classic Bikini, Size Small."

I was shocked. I had sent the wish list I had pre-pared for my mother to the entire RA staff! I thanked my staff member and immediately ran down to my room to send out the correct staff wish list with a nice little note, trying to make the best of my total embarr-assment. For the next few days, everyone mentioned my need for good underwear.

On the night of the Christmas party, everything went over perfectly. Everyone had opened their gifts and discovered the identity of their Secret Santa. Then, one of my fellow RA's stood up. "We have something for Molly, just to thank her for putting this whole party together." It was a pink box. I knew what it was immediately. My face turned beet red and I was laughing so hard my eyes were full of tears. I walked up to the front of the group, took the box, and was speechless. I opened up the box to see 10 pairs of neatly folded Victoria's Secret Classic Bikinis, all size small. All I could say was thanks. My friends had taught me a very important life lesson: always double-check your e-mail attachments.

Molly Elizabeth Kepley – Resident Assistant
North Carolina State University -
mekepley@unity.ncsu.edu

# Clearing the Air

I have been an R.A for only six months now, but I have filled out a massive number of incident forms in that short time. And as an RA for 60 freshmen, incidents are not always, if ever, what I would consider "normal." One of the funniest incidents I ever confronted occurred within the first three weeks of classes.

Being at a relatively small university in Iowa, we tend to attract many students from small farm towns. Not all of them have ever lived away from home or in a place when they have to lock their doors at night. As a precautionary measure, one of my residents (we'll call her Jennifer) received a container of pepper spray before she left for college, and she kept the container hanging on her key chain. One day, Trisha, from across the hall, wandered over to her neighbors' room to visit and curious, she picked up the pepper spray and, without asking, proceeded to spray the whole bottle out into the room. She said that she thought it was perfume or air freshener! Either way, the majority of the floor had to be evacuated and all the windows were opened for a higher level of ventilation. We followed this incident up with a program that had our Director of Security as our featured speaker, and I suppose it was a simple mistake for anyone to make, but I know I'll never forget it!

Dorothy Anello – Resident Assistant
St. Ambrose University - danello@hotmail.com

# Mr. Pigg

My residents are the best! During the first semester, after I had come back from a weekend at home, I realized that I left my favorite stuffed animal, Mr. Pigg at home! You need to understand, I sleep with this guy every night! I was really upset, since my mom refused to send him to me by anything other than the regular mail (no over night delivery or anything!!). I didn't know how I'd get to sleep until I got him back.

Once my residents found out that Mr. Pigg was MIA, they took action. While I was at class, they lined up all of their own favorite stuffed animals right in front of my door. There was a note on my wipe board saying, "Sorry Mr. Pigg isn't with you. Here are some of our stuffed animals; hope they'll do until Mr. Pigg gets back, safe and sound!"

That made my day, week, and month! I still have the pictures of all the stuffed animals. The funny thing was that on that particular day, our university was holding an open house and I was giving tours of our floor. Not only did I have to explain what was going on to the people who I was giving the tour to, but had to ask them to step over all the animals as well! It's one of my fondest memories. My girls are WONDERFUL!

Shelly Hopper, Resident Assistant
Eastern Illinois University -
cumdh@mail.pen.eiu.edu

# Lucky

Laughter has been the most beneficial tool in my experience as a Resident Assistant. Giggles have come in handy several times, but one particular situation stands out vividly in my mind. Announcements flooded the campus as news of an approaching Hurricane shook up the small town of Saint Leo, FL. This was a very common situation as the state of Florida is prone to hurricanes. I was a RA with first year female students. Naturally, my residents were feeling a bit terrified, but also apparent were their joy in the fact that classes were canceled until further notice.

Later on that day, the mood became calmer as whispers and giggles filled my hallway. I couldn't understand what exactly was fascinating my residents. I walked down the hallway and everyone said hello to me but no one looked me in the face, which was unusual. I decided to take a visit to the room, which seemed to be the "hot spot". I knocked on the door and guilty voices whispered, "Lynne's at the door. What are we going to tell her?" About five minutes later the door opened and about ten of my residents were stuffed into one room. Guilt dripped off of their faces but there was no sign of what exactly was going on. I questioned the girls and all they did was giggle. Suddenly, I heard an unfamiliar noise in the closet. I recognized the sound, but it was a sound that did not belong in the residence halls.

The girls all looked at each other as if they had already been busted. I slid open the closet door and out pounced a little gray and white kitten. "Girls" I said, "what is going on?" They all gazed at each other until one was brave enough to answer. "Well, we found this kitten outside in the parking lot and we didn't want to leave him outside because a hurricane is coming. So we saved his life!" I smiled at the girls and they all began to giggle. What else could I do but laugh?

Well, I told the girls that they could keep the kitten until the storm passed and then they had to find it a home. Needless to say, the next day we all awoke to a beautiful sunrise and to the good news that the hurricane had passed and spared us once again. I don't know exactly what happened to the precious kitten, but my residents will never forget him and they even named him "Lucky" as they are convinced that they saved his life. About one week later I came home and my residents had slid pictures of "Lucky" under my door with a note "Thanks for letting us keep Lucky, you're the best!" The story of "Lucky" the kitten will always live on at Saint Leo University and each time that I think of it I have to laugh. What else could I do but laugh?

Lynne Fraino – Resident Assistant
Saint Leo University - Lynne.Fraino@saintleo.edu

# Burning Down the House!

When I learned over the summer that I had been offered a position as a RA I was so excited. I had previously been chosen as an alternate and now I had a position on staff for the '99-00 year! I would be working with freshman, which I was looking forward to. However I had less then 2 weeks to get all of my stuff together for my SINGLE room! In a mad dash to get everything, I frequently visited the mall, Linens N Things, Wal-Mart, and all of the other college shopping stores. I decided that since I was going to have a single why not get some small appliances such as a sandwich maker and an air popcorn popper. I felt ready.

Not too long after my shopping excursions, I found myself at Lycoming College, a whole week early for RA training. Once I was in my room, I started to unpack and move-in, and within a few hours it was starting to look like home.

The next morning we had our first day of training. After a long and info-filled day I decided to reward myself with a nice hot buttery bowl of air-popped popcorn.... you know take my new popcorn maker out for a test pop. So I hooked it all up and turned on the machine, and since the machine was quite noisy I closed my door and continued popping. However, my excitement was cut off about 5 minutes later when the building fire alarm started going off, and security was evacuating the building. When I saw my new supervisor (in her Pj's and along with the rest of the RA staff) I informed her that I thought I had set off the building alarm. She said, "Room 105?" and I sheepishly replied, "yeah that's my room I was making popcorn."

Needless to say, I was the joke of the week, the new RA setting off the fire alarm. Still, I have not made popcorn since that famous time, and my air popcorn maker now resides in the closet.

Aaron Seiz - Resident Advisor
Lycoming College - seiaaro@lycoming.edu

*You're only human,*
*you're supposed to make mistakes.*
*-Billy Joel*

*The more I want to get something done,*
*the less I call it work.*
*-Richard Bach*

# You'd Think They Would Learn!

The following is a revised guide that I threw together the year before I became an RA. I wrote it up for a couple of my friends that were already RA's, by taking all of their complaints about the stupid stuff that some residents do and putting it to paper. I got the biggest kick out of the things people would attempt and I didn't really believe that they so totally lacked common sense. I was shocked when, just a year later, this same lack of common sense was tried on me too! It was after some of my own experiences that I threw a couple of my gems into the guide as well, resulting in the finished project.

### Drink Smart: A Guide for Freshmen (and Dense Upperclassmen Who Haven't Learned the Ins and Outs of Drinking Yet)

The best place to drink, besides at the Upper Classmen Dorms, is in your room with the door shut. Hang and play "cards" with your friends and roommates in your room, not in the common area. When you leave the dorms with an empty bag & come back with a square one (or a rattler), even an RA or desk attendant can guess that it's a 30 pack or bottles.

Try stocking up before the desk opens. Stay on top of empties. When RA's come around, you only have the one in your hand despite having the rest of the 12 pack in your stomach.

71

# InspiRAtion for RAs

Do **not** prop your common area door and drink out of a bottle out there: that's just downright stupid. Even more stupid, doing the above during the times that RA's do rounds. Duh. Know when your RA's do rounds and avoid much inconvenience.

Direct quote from the RA handbook: "RA's must knock and identify themselves as an RA." So ask who is it. You'll have approximately a minute to hide the beer. Use this time wisely. If more than one minute is necessary, and you're with mixed company or are out of the closet, yell "One minute while **WE** put our clothes on."

Keep beer and drugs well hidden, i.e. in your own personal trunk (they can't search in there). Drink out of a cup, RA's aren't supermen, but they can see though glass, so use colored plastic.

Even non-alcoholic beer is considered beer. Like you're drinking it anyway. And Yeah, I think they've heard the "It's apple juice!" or "It's only iced tea" ones before, too.

It's not a good idea to have your stereo loud enough for the other side of campus to hear; doing so is an open invitation for an RA to visit your room and find you drinking.

The 21+ floors are not a safe haven for under-aged drinkers. An RA lives there too, and other RA's are there at least twice as much as the normal apartments. If you must drink there and you're under-aged, keep the beer in front of someone over 21 when an RA goes through.

Even if RA's are your friends, if you do something stupid they have to write you up, especially if they're with other RA's.

If an RA is around, only a moron talks about buying beer or where the Phat parties are. And don't brag to RA's about being totally wasted, poo-poo-faced, blitzed, drunk, bombed, etc.

Do not follow RA's, Resident Directors and Campus Police into a rowdy situation, they document everyone in the place, including you, the moron, that follows them in.

Something I would suggest **not** doing: Breaking an alcohol bottle open to eat the crystals is a dumb idea in the first place, you're already drunk and will probably eat the broken glass too, but to break it on the RA's wall... I really don't know what to call someone that foolish.

It might be smart to not say all the four letter words to or about an RA, slam doors in their faces, threaten them, etc. The WILL enjoy slapping the big fine on you for "acting out" (a very flexible term).

If caught with a beer in hand, remember these sentences, "No, I do not have anymore beer. That was my last one."

# InspiRAtion for RAs

The paper you sign to live in the Residence Halls is not called the Constitution, it's called your "Housing Contract." Last I checked, under aged drinking wasn't a Constitutional right, so you got nothing. If you are civil with RA's, they are nicer to you, and will not write you up as much. Not to mention there is what is called a recommendation form."

If you are a jerk, they write you up for stupid stuff (like candles), and tell other RA's about you.
Good luck!

Jeffrey Kershaw – Resident Assistant
jeff15kersh@netscape.net

# Baptist Interviews

I am the Assistant Director of Residence Life at Baylor University. Baylor University is a school priding itself on its Christian mission. In doing so, Baylor strives to develop individuals into well-educated world leaders who have a strong Christian foundation. As part of my job, I oversee all student development efforts within the on-campus community, consisting of eleven residence halls housing approximately 3500 undergraduates. We hire eighty-eight undergraduate students who are proven leaders to live in the residence halls and provide leadership for our residents, and these students Resident Assistants.

In order to be selected as an RA, a student must, among other things, go through a panel interview conducted by myself and the Director of Residence Life, Mr. Jim Broaddus, three Hall Directors, and three or four current RAs who will be returning for another year. The interview lasts about fifteen minutes, but for the candidate, sometimes interviewing for their first "big" job, it seems much longer and to have to go before so many "important" adults, it is quite intimidating.

At our 1998 round of interviews, two students made impressions we've yet to forget! Mr. Broaddus usually goes to the lobby to escort the student candidate into the interview room. We are all seated around a long executive table. The candidate takes a seat at the head. I always sit closest to the candidate to explain the interview process and to begin. Mr. Broaddus had just escorted a candidate in and had introduced himself. As the candidate was seated, I introduced myself and the candidate asked, "Are ya'll (we are in the South) related?" I responded that no, I was Wallace and he was Broaddus.

Without missing a beat, the candidate looked straight at me and asked, "So, you are bra-less?" The room was very quiet and not one person made eye contact for the rest of the interview for fear of laughter. The candidate never even knew he had asked about my undergarments!

Not too long after that interview, came a young man who had listed the honor of Eagle Scout on his application. A fellow Eagle Scout was on the panel and one of his questions for the candidate was to relate some of the activities he had planned in order to receive his honor to the activities he would plan as a RA. Again, without missing a beat, the young man replied that he "had gained a lot of experience programming for large people." He had meant to say large groups of people, but we all had to wonder if he would plan things for the skinny people as well!

I'm happy to say that both of these young men are now on our staff and doing a great job! When we recently went through staff training, I gave away an award to anyone who would admit that they were the ones who made those statements. Neither of the young men even remembered the event because they were so nervous. But, we have all enjoyed their humor.

Elizabeth Wallace – Asst. Dir of Residence Life
Student Development Coord- Baylor University
Elizabeth_A_Wallace@baylor.edu

# Pager Go Down the Hole...

I was on-call one night and I had to do my business in the bathroom. At our school, we have to wear pagers while we're on duty and mine was clipped to the pocket of my jeans at the time. I did my thing, finished, flushed and pulled up my jeans.

"PLOP"

I turned around realized that my pager had slipped out of my pocket and into the flushing toilet! Luckily, the pager did not go down the "hole". Working myself into a frenzy, I quickly yanked it out after the toilet finished flushing, wiped it off, and ran to my room where I proceeded to spray about a ton of Lysol on it. After I set it aside to air-dry, I called the front desk to tell them that the "battery in my pager had gone bad" and that I would "be in my room for the rest of the night."

That night I did some serious praying. Luckily, everything turned out okay and the pager just fine worked the next morning with a "new battery." I was extremely relieved that I did not have to explain that the pager almost got flushed "down the hole."

However, this year we have all new pagers. I wonder what happened to the old one that I had?

Red Jordan – Resident Assistant
devilpup_25@yahoo.com

# Four

# Staff Support

"I was the first-ever Community Service Coordinator/ Building Director for the first-ever community special-interest residence hall on our campus last year. I was blessed with 40 amazing residents and two fantastic RAs to boot, and it is incredible what can be produced when you mix this small (but mighty!) group of people together in a building far from campus with this central interest of service. The closeness that emerged is immeasurable, and that closeness is the facet of this experience that will outlast all of the others."

Michelle Messersmith – Housing Coordinator
Allegheny College – messerm@alleg.edu


*Each friend represents a world in us, a world not born until they arrive, and it is only by this meeting that a new world is born. -Anais Nin*

# The Ties That Bind

Mallory Hall 1997-1998: We had a great staff that year. I've never felt a greater bond with 4 other women. Personality-wise, the five of us were from separate corners of the Earth. But somehow we all clicked and had many good times together. The year started off a little rocky since our personalities and work-styles were so dynamically different.

I was very uptight and organized. I demanded structure, and was not "touchy-feely" at all. Michele was older, she took things in stride and she was always hugging us - the maternal figure of the group. Jen flew by the seat of her pants, very carefree, passionate, and caring. And Sarah was a smart-alec, who went with the flow, but still liked a little structure. Our Hall Director, Alie, was wild, unstructured, and loved to have fun, but she also knew when to be mature.

Alie began to develop our staff from day one of training. During the first month, we all went canoeing together, cooked each other dinner, and could be found hanging out in one another's rooms at all times of the day and night. We also began to play harmless practical jokes on one another, a tradition which continued through the following April. Whether it was kidnapping Michele's bird and leaving a ransom note or the 4 others ganging up and decorating my door with 128 condoms, those light humorous moments were great for bonding. Throughout the year, we would continue to do staff development activities, not because it was "mandatory fun", but because we wanted to be together.

The residents of each floor knew the other RAs in the building too, because we were always on one another's floors. (Consequently, we often had to accompany one another to judicial hearings because we always seemed to encounter residents violating rules while we were cooking dinner, watching a movie, or hanging out on another's floor!) At the end of the year, we made a scrapbook of pictures, quotes, and inside jokes to commemorate our year together. I treasure that scrapbook.

Perhaps the big thing that made us so close was the fact that several of us faced some pretty rough times in our personal lives that year. We all stuck together, laughed together, and cried together. Only two months into the academic year, my father died and I went home for a week. While I was gone, my Hall Director and the other three R.As sent me flowers, and when I returned, they all greeted me within the hour. It was hard dealing with the death of my father with the rest of my family at home two hours away. My fellow staff members became a surrogate family for me and without their support and love, I don't know how I would have made it through that year. When I couldn't sleep, they stayed awake with me for hours on end. When I needed to talk, they listened. When I couldn't talk but needed companionship, they sat with me in comfortable silence. They understood when I was irritable and moody. They made me smile when not much else could.

## *Staff Support*

We all went our separate ways in May 1998: Michele and I went on to work in separate halls, Jen went to study abroad, and Alie and Sarah stayed in Mallory. We kept in touch last year and even had Mallory reunions. Alie and Sarah graduated last year but this year Jen returned and even though the three of us work in separate buildings, Jen, Michele, and I are like the Three Musketeers (or the Three Stooges at times!). Jen and Michele are two of my closest friends and I thank God that we were thrown together as staff members in 1997. I don't know what I'd do without them. Even though we get together almost once a week, we always reminisce about the good old days in Mallory Hall. It was a truly remarkable experience – in my 3 years working in residence life, I have never seen a closer staff.

Maybe it's the fact that we worked in the only non-coeducational hall on campus or the fact that we were the only all-female staff sets us apart and allowed us to be unique together. Or maybe it's the fact that opposites attract and though we were all so different, we managed to compliment each other to form a dynamic team. Nonetheless, we were 5 distinct women, who challenged and supported one another, who learned to be flexible with each other, and who had the times of our lives laughing, singing, and being a family as the women of Mallory Hall 1997-1998.

Karen McLaughlin – Administrative Coordinator
University of Florida – kamra@ufl.edu

# Muscular Dystrophy: A Positive Influence on Our Community

Muscular Dystrophy is an inherited disease that causes increasing weakness in muscle tissue. The primary muscles affected are skeletal muscles and occasionally, the muscles of the heart. There are nine different types of Muscular Dystrophy. In all of these different types of dystrophy, the muscle tissue seems to be affected in a random fashion. There is usually evidence of degeneration, and then regeneration of some muscle fibers. These muscles usually become larger than normal, and eventually are replaced by scar tissue and fat.

Although there are nine different forms of Muscular Dystrophy, the most common form is Duchenne Muscular Dystrophy. It occurs in one of every 3,300 male births, and usually occurs between the ages of two and six. Since it is a sex-linked disorder, it almost exclusively strikes males. A defective gene on the 23rd, or X, chromosome causes the disease. The muscle wasting progresses upward from the legs, and eventually the arms become affected. Finally, the muscle wasting affects the muscles of the diaphragm. Breathing becomes more difficult, and pulmonary infections become a constant hazard. These infections, coupled with respiratory failure, will often bring about death before the age of twenty.

There are not any obvious symptoms within

the first year of life. It is when the child first
starts walking that abnormalities begin to surface.
These abnormalities include frequent falling, a
difficulty in getting up from a sitting or lying position, difficulty climbing stairs, an inability to run,
and a waddling manner of walking. There are also
visible characteristics of this form of Muscular
Dystrophy, such as what appears to be an enlargement of the calf muscles. This enlargement
is really due to an accumulation of fat and con-
nective tissue in the muscle.

Muscular Dystrophy has directly affected
myself, as a Resident Assistant, and has directly
affected all members of the community in which I
live. This is due to the fact that one of our community members, Karim, suffers from Muscular
Dystrophy. Karim suffers from many of the elements listed above. He has difficulty climbing
stairs; he cannot run; he has difficulty standing
up from a sitting or a lying down position; he falls.
None of these elements stop him from succeeding.

Karim is very open about having Muscular
Dystrophy, and is in no way ashamed of himself
or of his condition. This openness has served as
the foundation for the fostering of community on
our floor. Each member of the community has
learned to accept others for who they are, as we
have all learned to see the inner person, the true
person inside of everyone. We have also learned
not to exclude anyone because they may be different, and we have come to the understanding that
everyone is unique in some way. No one in our
community is apprehensive to share what is
unique about himself. Because of my residents,

and especially because of Karim, I have learned how to put forth a college community based upon compassion, trust, and unconditional acceptance. This has led me to live my life based on these same values.

It has been my pleasure to see my community grow and mature throughout this school year. We have learned so much about ourselves, and we have learned so much from each other. I personally have learned something from each and every one of my community members. One of the greatest things I have learned is a lesson of courage. I must thank all of my residents for this, but I must especially thank Karim. His courage is incredibly, and faithfully strong. He is not afraid, and he possesses the conviction and the will to humble himself by trusting those around him. I have learned that a commanding community will ultimately encompass us if we walk humbly with one another, and if we trust those around us.

I did not teach my residents about building this trust and this community; they taught me. Their example, and their daily demonstration, made me aware of the 5-fold purpose of such a community: to teach, to learn, to listen, to encourage growth, and to join hands and live happily. Muscular Dystrophy may cause an increased weakness in muscle tissue, but it has not, and will not, cause an increased weakness in our community.

Andy Duran – Resident Assistant
St. Leo University -anthony.duran@saintleo.edu

# RA Unity

I started out my RA experience as a junior at Fordham University in the Bronx, NY. The people I interacted and worked with were my forty male residents, and my six co-workers, for a total of four males and three female R.As in our hall, all of us supervised by a graduate student R.D.

We were an incredibly tight group that really worked well together, no matter what we were doing. Whether it was dealt with handling a drunken student, or working together to present a program or arrange a speaker, we supported each other. The three senior R.As were great leaders for the four junior R.As – and above all else, you always knew that you were a part of the Finlay team. We had a real sense of pride for our residents and in our building. As a joke, we always used to say, "We're Finaly and you're not!"

All the other RAs around campus knew that we were the "cocky" or the "cliquey" staff, but it wasn't necessarily a bad thing. The closeness of our staff was something that other RA staffs were constantly striving for. Sure, we had our share of disagreements, but we always kept in mind that we had to remember the main goal - that of supporting each other, and serving the residents of our hall to the best of our ability.

The year after all of the seniors graduated, all four juniors stayed as R.As for another round. The RD moved to a different building, along with two of the juniors who had been in Finlay, and the other two of us stayed in Finlay. That fall, we all got together for a dinner in downtown NY. We sat around the table remembering the war stories of Finlay, the inside jokes, and our famous motto: "We're Finlay and you're not." To this day, we still keep in touch, and cherish the great team we had in Finlay Hall.

Sean Cryan
Director of Student Life Programming
King's College – sfcryan@kings.edu


*Friendship is the only cement that will
ever hold the world together.
-Woodrow Wilson*


*The way to make a true friend is to be one. Friendship
implies loyalty, esteem, cordiality, sympathy,
affection, readiness to aid, to help,
to stick, to fight for, if need be…
Radiate friendship and it will return sevenfold.
-B.C. Forbes*

# Making a Difference
# One Student at a Time

My housing career has been filled with positive interactions with Resident Advisors, Hall Council participants, residents, and countless others. When I reflect on the last few years, I always think of one moment that particularly made me feel like I had truly made a difference in someone's life. I think about my former Resident Advisor, Sherita.

Sherita was hired as a mid-year Resident Advisor in January of 1996. It was only my second semester working for housing as a Coordinator, and so it was the first time I actually hired a staff member and was responsible for the majority of her training. Sherita and I spent quite a few hours together over the first few days of her RA tenure going over policies, procedures, and paperwork. It was a learning experience for both of us! Being so new to housing, there were questions Sherita asked that I didn't even know the answers to myself. But we managed to get through the tough part and things went rather smoothly for the rest of the semester.

For the next two academic years, Sherita worked for me as an RA. Our relationship grew both professionally and personally. She always told me about the classes she was taking and how much she enjoyed her major. Sherita and I talked about her career goals, which included finding a job where she could incorporate her strong religious background. She also confided in me when her family was going through rough times, and I tried to help her find the time be with her family. When Sherita was in her last semester before graduation, she told me about her internship experiences at a juvenile training center for delinquent teens and how she knew she was doing the job meant for her.

As Sherita was preparing for graduation and trying to find a job in the "real world", we often talked about career-related topics such as resume writing, interviewing, and what types of questions to ask during the interview to get a good feel for the organization and the potential supervisor. Knowing Sherita for so long, I knew there were certain things that were important to her and I didn't want her to lose sight of them for the sake of taking the first job that came along.

Graduation came, and Sherita headed home. I thought about her often throughout the summer and wondered if she had found a job that would satisfy her and offer her a good experience. The new school year approached and I found myself sitting in my office once again during RA training. And then to my surprise, I got a phone call from Sherita. Naturally, I was thrilled to hear from her and hoped for good news.

Sherita did share with me her news - she had found a job working with juvenile delinquents in a Christian-based organization. The topper to the good news was that the job was in Wilmington, which is where she really wanted to be! She told me that she had blindly sent resumes out to organizations that may be able to offer her the type of job she was looking for. Before long, she had an interview and soon after, she had a job offer.

## Staff Support

During our brief conversation, Sherita told me that I was the first person she called after her parents. She wanted me to be one of the first people to know because I had been such a help to her during her college career.

She thanked me for understanding and supporting her, for the personal support, and the professional advice. Sherita also spoke about how being a
Resident Advisor had helped her beyond what she imagined. While working as an RA, she wasn't aware of how much she was learning about relating to others, how to work with a group of people, and how to relate to her supervisor. We had been through a lot together over our 2 ½ year work relationship.

Sherita's phone call was a great inspiration to me. I was honored that she wanted to share her good news with me and that I had made such a difference in her life. That one phone call helped me to believe that I am in the right profession. It is my hope that I make a difference in students' lives, but to get a great phone call like that helps me to understand that I am.

Heidi Bennekamper – Residence Life Coordinator
East Carolina University
bennekamperh@mail.ecu.edu

# Lifelines

A little over five years ago, when I was a sopho-more in high school, I was diagnosed with clinical depression and put on suicide watch. I attempted to kill myself on more than one occasion, but every time, I stopped myself because I started to remember all of the goals that I still wanted to reach, and all of the people I knew who cared for me and loved me. I received professional help from both psychologists and psychiatrists, and because of an endeavor to Italy upon which I received spiritual and mental help, along with personal growth, I have a greater respect for my own life.

I am now in my second year of college as a Resident Assistant at Saint Leo University in Florida. Except for some minor incidents of in-sanity due to the amount of work and responsibil-ity, I procured upon myself, and I would say that I had a fairly good handle on my life. But on Feb-ruary 15th, 2000 that wasn't the case.

I could feel it, the anxiety, the stress, the fear of not knowing what was going to happen next; it all started to build slowly over a period of time. I've been to counselors and psychologists and psychiatrists for many years and there was one thing I'll never forget them saying, TALK! They would tell me never to keep my emotions bottled up inside, it's not healthy. Talk to people. For some reason, I ignored that bit of information this time. I didn't talk with anyone; I let the power of unhealthy stress and anxiety takeover my body. I sat in my room and cried.

I started to question my importance, and myself. I thought about dying. At one point, I actually had a knife next to my arm, and the blade was touching my skin; however, I refused to apply any pressure. I sat there motionless as the tears streamed down my face. I felt lost, unloved, abandoned, and unwanted. Prior to that day, I had been praying for God to send someone new into my life, someone who would listen and understand. This was not unusual for me, because I am a very spiritual person. I always have been, and always will be. As I sat in the chair and cried, I begged for God to send me someone. After some time, all of the crying that I had done gave me a terrible headache, and eventually I fell asleep. The following day I woke with a better frame of mind, but I wasn't totally feeling better.

That afternoon as I walked out into the lobby of the building, my hall director Michael was standing at the desk. He asked me what was wrong, and said that he could tell something was going on, without me saying a word. I went into his office and sat down on the couch.

The phone rang, and while he took the call, I was preparing myself to tell him what was going on, but I wasn't sure how to say it. Michael hung up the phone and asked me again what was wrong, the concern for me showing in his voice. I told him in a somewhat sarcastic way that last night was an interesting evening. He started to guess what could possibly be wrong. I looked at him, and with all sincerity, simply stated that last night I had tried to kill myself.

# InspiRAtion for RAs

After I told him what had happened, a rainbow effect of praises occurred. Michael opened his heart and shared examples from his own life on how he deals with stress and anxiety. He told me how privileged he was to know me. He said that he was jealous of me and amazed that a person could have such a great passion for life, and is so devoted to their faith, their family, their friends, and themselves. If he could trade places with me in order to take away the pain that I've gone through throughout the years, he would. He reassured me that there wasn't anything that would happen in my life that would give me reason to kill myself. I have succeeded so many times in my past, and I'll do it time and time again, and I'll come out on top. My prayers have been answered. God placed someone new in my life, someone I can trust to be there. He reassured me that if I ever needed anything, never to hesitate to ask him. It doesn't matter if it's here, at school, or if he's back home in New York, and I'm wherever, he would be there in a second. I knew as soon as I met Michael at the beginning of the year, that our lives would have a profound impact on each other. I'm happy that we're friends, and we know that we can count on each other.

Bethany Smith – Resident Assistant
St. Leo University - goofbeth@hotmail.com

# My strengths, my coworkers, My FRIENDS

To the
Binnewies Hall Staff:

We were once strangers
With just a name and a face
We took one day at a time
As we entered this new place
The days continued on
New friendships began to form
The little things about each other
We all began to adore
It's amazing how life can be
How we were all forced together
But as our lives move on
We will be in each other's lives forever
I will always remember the times
Those in the past and those yet to come
The shoulders we had to cry on
The sad times and the fun
We have a whole year
To grow, to love, to give
And with each other's help
Our lives will be easier to live
So keep in your hearts our times together
That we all know will have to end
But never forget each other
We'll always be lifelong friends

# Inspi**RA**tion for RAs

I wouldn't be the person I am today if I had never met my fellow RA's. They are the people who were always there for me for support as well as for friendship. They helped me set goals, they helped me dream, and they helped me become who I am. I love each and every one of them dearly and I always know that our memories that we share will last a lifetime.

Regina Siemonsma – Resident Assistant
South Dakota State University
regina9@hotmail.com

*We cannot tell the precise moment when friendship is formed. As in filling a vessel drop by drop, there is at last a drop which makes it run over. So in a series of kindnesses there is, at last, one which makes the heart run over.*
*-James Boswell*

*Friendship is a plant which must be often watered.*
*-Anonomous*

# Wear Your Staff Shirts

As you will probably realize, it is a takeoff on the Baz Luhrmann "Everybody's Free (to Wear Sunscreen)."

Hey Russell Complex, Hope this keeps you laughing as the year gets rough...

Ladies and gentlemen of the staff of 99/2000: Wear your staff shirts. If I could offer you one tip for the coming week, staff shirts would be it. The longtime benefits of fashion unconscious staff shirts have been proved by your professional staff, whereas the rest of my advice has no basis more reliable than my own meandering experience. I will dispense this advice now...

Enjoy the power and beauty of your bulletin boards. Never mind. You will not understand the power and beauty of your bulletin boards until they've been ripped down some night by a drunken fool believing themselves to be Hurricane Harrington. But trust me. In 24 hours you'll think back on how much time you spent on them and recall in a way you can't grasp now how much possibility laid before them and how fabulous they really looked. You are not as creatively challenged as you imagine. Don't worry about programming. Or worry but know that worrying is as effective as trying to hold a binge drinking prevention program by calling the liquor store. The real troubles in your life are apt to be things that never crossed your worried mind - the kind that bring Public Safety to your door at 4am asking if little Johnny is one of your residents. Do one thing everyday that scares your CC. SING. Don't be reckless with your KBR's. We will not put up with people who are. MEDITATE. RAs don't waste your time on jealousy. Sometimes you're your Hall Director's favorite and sometimes you're not. The year is long and in the end, eh, you're only one of the little people anyway (he he).

Remember your residents' names, forget the names they call you. If you succeed in doing this, tell me how. Keep your old program purchase receipts; throw away your old bank statements (there's no money in the account anyway). SCREAM. Don't feel guilty if you don't know what to do in a crisis. The best RA's I know didn't know at 2am who to call for a 2 alarm lounge blaze. Some of the absolute best RA's I know still don't. Get plenty of counseling. Be kind to your custodians - you'll miss them when they're gone. Maybe you'll document. Maybe you won't. Maybe you'll hold successful programs. Maybe you won't. Maybe you'll get a promotion. Maybe you'll do the pony dance in front of your entire complex staff. Whatever you do, don't assign blame - or take it either. Your mistakes will be pinned on your supervisor. So will everybody else's. Enjoy your Director. Use her every way you can. Don't be afraid of her or of what other people think of her. She's the greatest boss you'll ever have. DANCE. Even if you have nowhere to do it but in your own staff meetings. Read the student handbook, even if you don't follow it. Do not read student surveys, it will only get you fired. Get to know your Area Coordinators - you never know when they'll be called something else.

## Staff Support

Be nice to your facilities people. They're your best link to your building and the ones most likely to fix your toilets when they won't stop flushing. Understand that decent grades will come and go, but a precious few A's should hold on. Work hard to bridge the gap between academics and the job. There is no RA class next semester. Live on West Campus once. But leave before it makes you hard. Live on East Campus once. But leave before it makes you... soft. PRAY. Accept certain inalienable truths: students will screw up, faculty will cancel, and you too will get apathetic. And when you do, you'll fantasize that when you were offered the job, "Students were angels," "faculty was reliable," and "freshmen respected their RA's." HD's, respect your RA's. Don't expect anyone to support you more. Maybe you have a great AC, maybe you baby-sit Chuck's children, but you never know when a disgruntled RA might rear their ugly head. Don't mess TOO much with your Hall Government, or by the time the end of the year rolls around, it has become Hell Government. Be careful which staff member's advice you buy, but be respectful of those who supply it. Advice is a form of therapy. Dispensing it is a way of fishing the past years from the disposal, wiping them off, painting over the ugly parts (usually 3 to 4 coats) and recycling it to save some young lives.

...But trust me on the staff shirts.

Lindsay Auten – Hall Director, Russell Hall C
University of Delaware – lint@Udel.Edu

# Just Like Spice

Just about a month and a half after opening in the fall, one of my ten RAs decided that it would best for him to resign. My staff was a little shocked by this and as you might assume, we discussed our loss in the next staff meeting. Each staff member spoke up about his or her feelings regarding our former co-worker's departure. Everyone recognized and understood that it was best for him and we knew that we just had to move on. And then a comment that RA Mike Neeves said summed it all up (and left all of us in complete uproar). He said, "Well, the way I see it is that we are kinda like the Spice Girls... Ginger Spice left but, we're going to be okay and we're gonna make another even better album... and Ginger is going to go on to something else and do well at that."

Jamie Hoffman – Graduate Hall Director
Arizona State Univ. – hoffman7@mainex1.asu.edu

*You have to take it as it happens, but you should try to make it happen the way you want to take it.*
*-Old German proverb*

*Better to bend than to break.*
*-Scottish proverb*

# Behind Closed Doors

During our week-long summer training, we went through a section called "Behind Closed Doors". BCD was the most feared and the most intense part of training, and we all knew this. I was a rookie and was one of the first groups of 4 to go through the series of simulations in BCD.

BCD simulations were high intensity situations that we may have to face on duty and in our residence areas. Some of the situations included: suicide threat, drug abuse, domestic violence, and 'coming out' aggressions. Acting in these scenarios, were the veterans, whom we just began to bond with.

BCD is a role-play, as if we are doing rounds. Every few rooms had a "problem" in it, and each group member took turns. To fully understand my situation, you need to know what I went through my freshman year.

In the fall of that year I met a girl named Meg. Meg put me through an extremely emotionally abusive relationship and on more than one occasion she even physically threatened me. This abusive relationship ended when she threatened suicide and was forced to leave school. In her note, she blamed me for all her problems. Needless to say, this caused me a great deal of emotional distress. After she left school, I went through a few difficult months, where I believed it had been my fault. I still thought about it a lot.

My BCD group had been through several simulations so far, a domestic assault, and an international student roommate conflict. It was my friend John's turn, and the three other members were observing. The four of us entered a dark room, with Sarah McLachlan's 'Angel' playing. In the corner was a senior member of my staff, Dave, in the fetal position. You could feel the tension in the room as each one of us rookies realized what this simulation was to entail – the threat of suicide.

John was my best friend; he had helped me through everything the previous year, and I was thanking God that it wasn't my turn in the simulation. John began to talk with Dave and Dave began to act like he was on Broadway. Instantly I began to have flashbacks of the previous semester, and I began to cry. I didn't know why, but I was determined to stay in the room. I began to hyperventilate and had to leave.

I was so embarrassed. One of the Hall Directors came and spoke with me. He knew all about Meg, and he understood what I was going through. I was exempt from that part of training. In the months that followed, I put the incident behind me and chose to ignore it; but in the back of my mind, I feared I might not be able to deal with a similar situation if it arose in my residence hall. And in December, my fears were confronted.

Throughout November, the room next to mine was very into WWF Wrestling, and I constantly heard thudding. I assumed that they were merely wrestling. But one night in early December, I learned that they were not wrestling, but actually fighting. Two of my male residents were fighting in their room on a regular basis. One of the residents, Mark, was constantly physically abusing the other.

I called Mark out to talk and he was rather open and was very emotional. He told me that he was seeing a psychologist and also on a fairly regular basis caused physical damage to his own body. After diffusing the situation and informing the appropriate people, I sat in my room and cried. I was not going to be able to deal with this. I sat and shook like a child. All I could think was, "My fears were right, in training I was afraid I wasn't going to be able to help one of my residents and now I cant... I hate Meg for what she has done to me! Who knew I wouldn't be able to help two of my OWN residents who live next door! WHY?!"

Kimmy, a fellow RA in the building, and one of my good friends and I talked. She informed me that I was not alone. I had a staff of 6 people who loved me and would back me up. It hit me light a bolt of lightning I was not alone, I had people behind me, and I did not have to carry the burden by myself. I will never forget what she said to me, "This staff was put together for a reason. Each one of us brings something different. Along with what we bring, we have our weaknesses too. I have my weaknesses, and with my weaknesses being offset by your strengths we are a awesome staff. You aren't expected to deal with everything alone. That's why I am here talking to you right now..."

Thank you, Kimmy, thank you.

\*\*Names have been changed to ensure privacy

Matt Gibson – Resident Assistant
Stonehill College - gibby320@hotmail.com

# Rebuilding Together

In my years as a Resident Assistant, I have always known the support and friendship shared by our staff. However, this year, I have realized the strength that each of us gives each other in times when everyone is at a loss for words.

This past fall, three of our residents were killed in an accident at another school while crossing the road coming from a party. Two of the freshman girls were roommates. Most of the residents of our hall did not know it happened until the next day, but when word got out that night, we all knew that we would have to deal with a lot of pain and grief, and that for the time being, we had to put our own emotions aside to help the girls we serve. One of the Resident Assistants on staff was a resident of my own from the previous year, and the other was a good friend of mine that was a second year RA. The returning RA had heard the news the night before, but my old resident had no idea what had happened, or that it had affected two of her girls. I knew that I had to stay in the lobby and wait for her to come back from being out of town, and we dreaded the news that we had to tell her. As soon as she got in we rushed her into a secluded room and told her what had happened.

It almost killed me to see her buckle down when we told her the bad news— it was bad enough that the three girls had lived in our residence hall, but to lose two of your own can be nothing short of devastating. I gave her a hug,

102

and tried to come up with something to tell her when she asked, "What do I do? What do I tell my girls?" The only thing I could say was "I don't know, I don't know." In my three years of being a RA, I had never gone through something like this, and I had no clue on how to handle the grief of over four hundred freshman women.

That day and the next, our hall was bombarded with the press looking for pictures, quotes, and memories of the girls who were killed just two days before. With the help of the university public relations department and many of our own staff, we were able to give the residents who knew the girls some time to get over the shock and then we were able to give the press some info about how we felt concerning the loss of three of our residents. However, overall most of the RAs, myself included, were still in shock. We simply could not believe that this could happen.

A few weeks later, when the hall was just starting to get back to normal, the RAs got together for a gripe session. Tensions had been running on high since the three deaths, and most of us were near the breaking point. After a few things were said, one of the RAs that had supervised one of the girls who had died spoke up. She explained how much she had not been able to grieve the loss on her own because she was trying to be strong for the families, her residents, and even the staff. She expressed that she was so stressed out that she had no idea on how to begin to grieve over her own loss.

Many of us were silenced - we had focused so much on how we had gotten on each other's nerves that we hadn't really dealt with the things that were really needed to strengthen the staff. From then on it became evident that we needed to listen to each other— not just to what was said, but to what was left unsaid as well. It became an unspoken decision to make sure that each person of the staff was supported, whether it was when one of us had the flu to dealing with the loss of a loved one or resident.

Our residence hall is still healing from the wounds of losing some of our own, but it has helped us realize that life is too short and precious to not support each other fully. This support has given us a new life, and has made us focus more on others than ourselves.

Jennessa Reed – Resident Assistant
Baylor University – jennessa_reed@baylor.edu

*This too, shall pass.  –William Shakespeare*

*Pain is never permanent. –St. Teresa of Aliva*

# It's When Things Seem Worse that You Must Not Quit.

One of the most important and life changing decisions I have made to date was when I decided to become a Resident Assistant. I was a foreign exchange student, a freshman from Nigeria, and I felt that the experience would be a good stepping-stone towards improving my communication and social skills in an environment that I was unfamiliar with. Most of all, I just wanted to be understood and accepted, but that would take over two years to achieve.

After going through my university's tedious carousel-like selection process, I became one of the twenty-two R.A staff members for the 1997-1998 academic year at Thomas Jefferson Residence Hall, University of Missouri-Rolla.

My first semester as an R.A, I went all out and had a small program for my floor almost every week. My first few weeks were very successful. I was able to get all of my freshmen to the semester's opening activities and they were all very excited. But later in the semester, things began to change. As with every community, there comes a time when people just stop being nice to each other and they start getting real. This is a movement from the "pseudo-community" stage to the "Chaos stage." The "community stage" was to come much later. Although I still made sure I knocked on everyone's door before a program, very few people were responsive. They seemed to have formed their own interests and cliques and no matter what kind of program I did, I could never quite reach them. I couldn't help thinking that there was something I wasn't doing right, or that they just didn't like me anymore. Things got worse when one of my residents, Jennifer wrote a letter to my supervisors, saying that I was an inadequate R.A. who didn't know my residents and that other residents on the floor felt the same way. I could find no reasonable explanation for this since I was doing everything an R.A. was expected to do and I was hurt that she didn't come to talk to me first; that she never gave me suggestions on what she would like to see me do.

I was on the verge of quitting when I decided to get advice from a senior staff member, Anita, who was in charge of the other wing. She told me that there would always be difficult and discouraging residents and that I was doing an incredible job. She gave me examples of similar experiences that she and other R.As had been through, and she told me how they managed to stick it through, even to the point of getting promoted! I realized how these obstacles made stronger R.As and how coping and sticking it out would help me in the long run. That was all I needed to keep me going.

The next semester, I got my residents to brain-storm some programming that they would like to see that semester, and I asked them to volunteer to organize those programs. I also asked my floor officers to write their expectations of me, and I did the same for them. Then we had weekly meetings to help assure us that we were staying on task and to discuss any floor business. In addition, we went over comments and suggestions from the

comment box that I placed outside my door. This
let the residents could be anonymous and honest
and all of these new approaches greatly improved
my community. But I still didn't feel that I had
the best relationship with every resident. Some of
my residents actually complained to my resident
director that I was trying too hard! I knew I could
not please everyone, so I continued to do my best
by doing less and getting my residents to do more.
I knew I did the best job as an RA that semester. I
did so well and I felt so good about myself that I
performed my best academically, produced four
R.As from my community, and to top it off, we
won community of the year that semester. As a
result, I was not surprised when I was listed on
the programming hall of fame and promoted to
senior resident assistant for the 1998-1999 academic year.

That next year, I was put on a floor of mostly
seniors, a new challenge since I was used to working with freshmen. That year, I focused more on
building personal relationships, hall-wide programming and letting the floor run itself. Of
course I got comments like, "She's doing so much
for the halls but nothing for the floor" but I had
learned my lesson. I formed new positions on the
floor so that everyone who wanted to be involved
on the floor had an opportunity. It was a good
system.

I faced other challenges that semester as an
RA, personally, and academically. Being so far
away from home was beginning to take its toll on
me, but I never quit. That year the community
produced one RA, Gina, who held one of the posi-

tions I created. Tina, one of the more creative residents and our social chair, became resident of the year, and she is planning on becoming an RA next year.  But the highlight of that year was at the end, when one of the first year R.As, named Henrietta, (one of the residents from my previous community) came up to me and said that she was sorry for being so hard on me when she was my resident.  She said that now she understood how much hard work it was to be an RA and that I was great and she was glad that she didn't have any residents like herself.

Today, as the Head Resident Assistant of Thomas Jefferson Hall for the 1999-2000 academic year, I supervise twenty-one Resident Assistants. I have earned several leadership awards from the university and I was featured in the October 1999 issue of Glamour Magazine as one of the Top 10 College women in the United States.  In May 2000, I will graduate with honors and move on to medical school. Rich with experience, I am able to give advice to all the R.A.s that come to me with various situations.  I tell them several of my experiences, and encourage them to never quit because if I had quit 2 years ago, I would never have made it this far.

*Names have been changed to protect the privacy of individuals.

Abere Karibi-Ikiriko – Head Resident Assistant
University of Missouri – Rolla - abkaribi@umr.edu

# This is Who I Am

My story is a heart warming one, actually a bit of a confidence builder I suppose.  During the 1998-1999 academic year, I was a new RA.  I was excited, anxious, and a little scared all at the same time.  My floor was a smaller community with only 14 residents.  They were all freshmen, which was conducive to a really tight community that I discovered early on was going to be both a blessing and a challenge.

Concerning the qualifications for the position, I knew I was a good candidate.  I'm outgoing, friendly and professional.  I was involved with many organizations on campus ranging from academia to the fine arts and I was pretty well known and respected on campus.  At a glance, it seemed that I had all of the perfect qualities for a good RA.  But there was one drawback:  one characteristic that I knew could be a major hurdle.  I am gay.

My supervisors didn't see it as a problem and neither did any of my contemporaries, and though I was "out" and comfortable in my sexuality, I wasn't as confident that my residents would be as comfortable or accepting.

A week before the freshmen arrived I began to plan my opening floor meeting.  What would I say?  I would lay down discipline rules, talk about programs and get ideas, tell them about my role as a confidant and listener... but should I open the closet doors right away or let them figure it out?  I've never been a gay advocate.  I've always viewed myself as a human being first and foremost and my sexuality doesn't make me who I am, only who I choose to love. But confidence will make others confident. If I showed that my sexuality wasn't a secret or an obstacle then they wouldn't see it as such either. However, if I jumped right out with it they would think it was the prominent feature of my personality and I would be viewed as their "gay" RA. I decided to keep quiet, but dropped a hint when I mentioned during the hall meeting that I would not stand for any prejudice or racist remarks. I stressed that the floor and the residence hall would be a respectful environment. I said I didn't want to hear racist remarks, religious slander or the word "fag". I think I got my point across.

A couple weeks into the year things were going well. A resident came to me one day and we were talking in my room. Then he saw a picture of my boyfriend and at first, I got embarrassed and a little nervous. I didn't want to scare my residents away. He asked me if that was my boyfriend. I said after a short pause "yeah." And then he said, "Cool. I thought he might have been since he's over here so much. You guys look good together."

That comment opened up over an hour of conversation, where I learned the whole floor had figured it out and that I was the only one in the dark!! He told me no one that he knew of on the floor had a problem and that everyone seemed cool with it. That took a load off of my shoulders and gave me a boost of confidence.

Throughout the year we formed a tight bond that has lasted to this day, of which I am very grateful for. They gave me a boost of self-esteem that made having an all new hall (and a much larger one, 57 students now) a lot easier this year.

## *Staff Support*

On our campus two current RAs and an Area Coordinator give the first round of RA interviews for new positions. In one of the interviews, of which I was not involved, a young woman interested in a position was asked what inspired her to seek out the position of an RA. She said "Rob Crowley. When the guys on his floor first got to the school they were a little weary of his sexuality. I guess many of them had never been exposed to it. At first they were distant from him but after a little while he, being the person he is, changed their minds. He made them realize who he was as a person and in doing that changed their minds about homosexuality over all. I really respect that. I want to be able to influence people and broaden their opinions about social issues in the same respect." The Area Coordinator involved with that interview and both the RAs all told me that conversation at separate times because all 3 had known about my initial fears going into the school year. As a side note, the interviewee ended up making a fine RA as well, I dare say!

It's an incredible feeling knowing you've opened someone's eyes. Though I'm not an advocate for homosexuality, as I mentioned, I AM an advocate for humanity and open-mindedness in all aspects of the word and I'm glad my presence in their lives was strong enough to undo what 18 years of social stigma had conditioned. And it's funny the feeling of completion and accomplishment you get from helping someone else.

Rob Crowley – Resident Assistant
ranews@roanoke.edu

## Chapter 5

# Acts of Kindness & Life Moments

*Scatter seeds of kindness everywhere*
*You go;*
*Scatter bits of courtesy - watch them*
*Grow and grow,*
*Gather buds of friendship, keep*
*Them till full-blown;*
*You will find more happiness than*
*You have ever known.*
*-Amy R. Raabe*

# The Quilt

I have been a R.A. for three years now, and every year, the job has progressively gotten better. Right now, I work specifically with freshmen, a wonderful group of people. They are so energetic and fired up to be in their first year of college. I see so many young men and ladies that have the potential to do so much.

As it goes, last year after the Christmas Break, a lot of "my girls" (as I like to call them) came back a little disappointed due to their grades. The community atmosphere among all of them seemed to be down. When I talked to some of them, I found that many had lost a lot of their self-confidence, and that they just felt down in general. It was like a spreading disease within the hall.

I knew that I had to do something, and the more I thought about it, I figured that the best thing that I could do would be to try to give them a little piece of something positive. I know that I can't change the world, but sometimes it's the little things in life that can make one smile. I did something very simple... I created a bulletin board.

Taking the time to put all of my emotions into the project, I patched pieces of construction paper on the board and when I was done, I wrote down a little saying that had come to me while I worked...

# InspiRAtion for RAs

## "The Quilt"

One patch all alone carries its own personality...

Two single patches sewn together create a bond
between two, quite like a friendship.

Three, four, so many more -
patches sewn together, they have the power to:
Love and care, Warm and share,
Quilt and comfort...

Many single patches sewn together create the
comfort that we share.

After writing "The Quilt" on the board, I stood
back to survey my work, and I thought that it still
looked empty. The final touch was adding all the
names of my girls, in shapes of patches. I loved it!

So many of my girls loved what I had done, and
I saved it for the new group of girls that I have this
year. It's awesome to see everyone looking for her
name or reading "The Quilt". I've been told that
it's a little piece of inspiration to some... knowing
that is enough for me. I can truly say that I've
made them stop and think... and maybe even
smile, something that I believe to be positive.

Shannon McGouirk – Senior R.A.
West Georgia University - stu5546@westga.edu

*Everyone needs help from everyone.*
*-Bertolt Brecht*

# Memories Never Fade...

In 1974, I entered graduate school at the University of Alabama. I had previously lived in the residence halls as an undergraduate at Ohio University, but I had never had I served as a Resident Assistant. When I entered graduate school, I learned that the housing office was seeking R.A's so I applied and received a position. I had a floor of freshmen and the experience was truly positive. Like many R.A's, I had a wing of fun and active young men, and I built wonderful memories with each and every one of them.

After a year, I graduated and moved back to Ohio where I worked as a guidance counselor. But three years later, I decided to return to the field of higher education, where I have been employed in the housing and residence life field since 1978.

In 1992, after moving back South, my wife and I were shopping in a mall in Birmingham, wen I was approached by a gentleman who inquired if my name was Gary Kimble. I answered that it was, and he replied that although I probably did not remember him, he remembered me because I had been his freshman RA seventeen years earlier. He went on to tell me that he had had a great time living on our floor and how much he had appreciated what I had done to make his first year at Alabama fun and meaningful. Although I did not recognize the gentleman at first, when he told me his name, the memories came flooding back. I even remembered where he lived on my floor and we talked about some of the other guys who had lived around his room. Needless to say, my wife was quite surprised by the conversation, and she was touched by what she heard.

To say the least, I was honored that this man had taken the time to approach me. The entire experience was so emotional for me. We often believe that what we do as residence life staff makes a difference and that it is meaningful. Sometimes, we are able to see the direct benefits of our interventions but often, we don't receive the feedback that reinforces those beliefs. This was a rare occasion and although it arrived seventeen years later, its meaning was certainly not diminished by time.

Gary Kimble, Associate Director of Residence Life
The University of Southern Mississippi –
Gary.Kimble@usm.edu

*The service we render others is the rent*
*we pay for our room on earth.*
*Wilfred Grenfell*

# Christmas Surprise

The best RA story I have to share happened during my second year as an R.A. Right before the holiday season, I sent letters home to each of my residents' parents stating that I was going to have a Christmas party on my section. I asked each resident's parents to send a present to their daughter in care of me. To make it easy, I requested that the gifts cost less than $10.00. I also impressed that the gifts were going to be a surprise and I requested that they help me keep the secret. And when the gifts stopped rolling in, I had received 100% presents from the parents.

It was so nice receiving all the presents – all twenty-five! My residents had no idea, so when I had a "MANDATORY CHRISTMAS PARTY" they came running and just about lost it! You should have seen the looks on their faces when they realized that the presents I handed out were from their parents or special loved ones. Some of the residents even said "Molly, that was so sweet of you to buy us all these presents and wrap them in different wrapping paper. And I swear, my mom has that same wrapping paper at home!"

What a fun event to get into the Christmas spirit and the neat thing was some of the parents even sent me a little gift or a thank you card!!!!! I know my residents will always remember that party, and so will I.

This is one of the reasons I love being an RA!!
Molly O'Leary – Resident Assistant
St. Mary's College – olea6627@saintmarys.edu

# Reversed Roles

Being a R.A isn't always about what you do for your residents, but also about the things that they do for you.  One night I was extremely sick, running back and forth from the bathroom all night long, and it was absolutely horrible.  All I wanted to do was go home and have my mom watch over me.  But it turned out I didn't need my Mom – I had my floor.

My residents would see me walking down the hall and they'd ask if I was all right and to call on them if I needed anything.  One student even watched over me while I was in the bathroom to make sure I didn't need her help.  Another student told me to keep my door cracked open that way she'd hear me call for help if I needed it and she even put one of the trashcans in my room (although I had to remove it later though because it smelled too bad!).

It made me realize how much they cared for me – just as much as I care for them - and that made me feel wonderful.  That night has given me an even greater respect for my residents than I already had.  Now I know I can count on them if I need their help.

Fawn Matlack – Resident Assistant
fawnmm@hotmail.com

*Wherever there is a human being,*
*there is an opportunity for a kindness.*
*-Marcus Annaeus Seneca*

# My Best Program

I used to think that the success of a program depended on the number of people who attended it. But in my 3rd year as an RA I found out that was not true at all....

I did a program called "Sarah Speaks Out (Sarah standing for "students against rape and harassment") and I put hours of work and dedication into it. And when it was time to present it, only person came.

At first I was disappointed, but that was only until we began the program, I discovered that the one person who had taken the time to attend had just been recently raped herself. She felt that it was her fault, and that there was nothing that she could do... but after talking with the presenter, myself and another RA, she seemed to finally understand that it could never be her fault, and that there were things she could do to begin the healing process.

It was at that point that I realized that these programs are not just a part of a job, not just something that we have to do, but that we can use them as a part of the job that we do for others... I think about that resident a lot and to me, touching her and helping her made Sarah Speaks Out one of my most successful programs ever.

Kimberly Larson – Resident Assistant
The Savannah College of Art and Design

# What Every College Creed Ought To Be

**Students are...**

...important people on this campus.

...not cold enrollment statistics,
but flesh & blood human beings with
feelings & emotions like our own.

... not to be tolerated so that we can
do our own things.
THEY ARE OUR THING

....not dependent on us.
Rather we are both
interdependent upon one another.

...not an interruption of our work,
but the purpose of it.
Without students there would be
no need for this institution.

Tony D'Angelo
Tony@Collegiate-EmPowerment.com

*If you are interested in purchasing "What Every College
Creed Ought To Be" in poster format, please contact:
The Collegiate EmPowerment Company
by calling toll free at 1-887-338-8246,
or email info@Collegiate-EmPowerment.com.

# Reaching Out

My first few weeks as a Resident Assistant at West Chester University were disappointing to me. The job was not what I had envisioned it to be. I imagined that I would be the oldest and that everyone would come to me with all of his or her problems. I was a junior psychology major and I was hoping to gain some experience counseling by helping my residents adjust to life on campus. Instead of feeling helpful, I was intimidated by my residents. Almost half of my floor were upper-class students and most were older than me. I felt like my floor would never need me; even the freshmen were independent and had their friend base established.

In an attempt to reach out to my residents, I visited their rooms to see how their classes were going. I was almost finished with my floor when I knocked on Megan and Caroline's door. They were freshmen and had known each other prior to coming to college. I never really saw them since they were both on the women's basketball team and practice demanded most of their time. They spent their weekends at home in New Jersey, so I had written them off as nonexistent residents.

When I knocked on their door, Megan answered. I asked her how things were going and suddenly, she broke down. It turned out that she and Caroline were thinking of dropping out of school. They told me about how difficult basketball was and how much they missed home. They had not made many friends in the hall due to

121

their busy schedule during the week and their trips home on the weekends. Together we sat in their room discussing everything that was making them so upset. Megan and Caroline cried and I felt helpless. I urged them to stick it out; I did not want to lose them as residents. I knew some student athletes who were able to manage the rigorous training schedule and their academics. I promised them that I would get my friends to talk to them about how they balanced athletics and academics. I pleaded with them to stay on cam-pus for the weekends to see what it was like and to try to make friends. I explained that many activities occurred on the weekends and that it would give them an opportunity to meet people. I managed to get them to promise to stay on cam-pus for the upcoming weekend and to set up a time when they could talk to my athletic friends.

I felt a mixture of emotions after leaving the room. I was glad that they could talk to me about their issues, but I was worried that I would fail them. In my heart I knew that dropping out or transferring was not the answer, but I did not want to force it on them. If they left, I knew that I would feel like a failure. I hoped that they would give West Chester a chance and fall in love with the University as I had my freshman year.

I periodically checked in on Megan and Caroline during that week. I introduced them to their floor mates and gave them ideas about things to do on the weekend. My athlete friends spoke to them about the benefits of being a college athlete and about time management. They stayed on campus for the weekend and when I approached them about their status as students, they said that they were giving West Chester a chance.

I became more comfortable as a Resident Assistant and with my floor as the semester continued. My residents no longer intimidated me and I felt like I was helping people. I always checked on Megan and Caroline. Soon, I did not have to question them about their plans; I knew they were going to stay. As the year progressed, my floor became a community and I loved my job.

The next year I was moved to a different floor, but Megan and Caroline stayed in the same room. I still checked in on them every once in a while just to make sure they were okay. As my senior year waned, I began to explore my future options. I applied to graduate school at a number of Philadelphia area universities and I decided to apply to West Chester as well. In the spring I was delighted to find out that I was accepted to West Chester's counseling program. I was also offered a live-in graduate assistantship for housing. After much deliberation I decided to stay at West Chester.

For the next two years I worked on my masters and was employed in housing. I lived in a Residence Hall on the other side of campus, but I did not lose track of Megan and Caroline. I ran into them all over campus and I always received updates on their progress.

I received my master's degree from West Chester University on May 3, 1998. As I prepared for the commencement ceremony, I saw something that brought tears to my eyes. Standing before me, in their caps and gowns, was Megan and Caroline. These two women who were determined to leave school and move home four years prior, were now receiving their bachelors degrees. Not only were they successes academically, but they had stayed with basketball and were the team's co-captains. I could not have been more proud.

To this day I keep a picture of Megan, Caroline and myself in my office. Whenever I feel down or feel like I am not making a difference, that picture serves as a reminder to me that sometimes it takes four years to see the product of your help. I know that it is rare to even witness such an event. I recognize how lucky I am to have been able to see two students succeed and to know that I had something to do with that success.

Megan Cahill – Resident Assistant
West Chester University - MCahill@admin.fsu.edu

*Unless we give part of ourselves away,*
*unless we can live with other people and understand*
*them and help them, we are missing the most essential*
*part of our own lives.*
*-Harold Taylor*

# The North Hall Boys

The North Hall Boys. This is how we're known around our campus. Everywhere we go and everyone we see, they all know us by name. It means something. It means something not only to the people who see us, or to those who hear us shout our name across campus, but to those who fall into our group; it means friendship and family. For one hundred plus boys, away from our families, some for the first time, it means security and that we are accepted. The name of North Hall Boys is not just a name, but it is a real way of life.

It all started the fall of 1999, when I came back as the only returning member of our Resident Assistant staff. I was given the opportunity to speak to the freshmen that would be residing in North Hall. This would kick off their introductory week of college through a program our university offers called M.A.S.T.E.R. Plan. We all met in our Recreation Room downstairs. Almost a hundred guys were packed in like sardines in a room, scared to death, and they anticipated my words. I stood up, introduced myself, and the words began to flow.

It wasn't as though I was speaking to them, but rather that they were taking in my words of encouragement and wisdom. They were listening to every word that I had to say. I talked about policies; I talked about rules; I talked about what the week was going to be like; and then I talked about the North Hall Boys.

125

# InspiRAtion for RAs

I began sharing with them what being a "North
Hall Boy" meant to me. The words family, commitment, and friendship, all came into my speech.
I spoke for about ten minutes and when I was
finished, I looked at the faces staring back at me.
No one spoke. I had worked up to this huge cli-
max about how I had made myself successful
through counting on my friends, and how I had
built a family within all of us residing in North
Hall, and you could have heard a pin drop. I told
them that they had to set the tone, that it was up
to them right now whether they were going to be
successful. Still there was silence, and I stood
everybody up and spoke, "All right fellas, repeat
after me... North Hall Boys, North Hall Boys..."

They followed! That night in a small non
air-conditioned room one hundred men who were
less than confident when they walked into that
recreation room, were now secure and more confident, as they chanted our name in unison. The
walls shook and the glass rattled! You could look
around that room and see the excitement in the
expression on everyone's face; you could feel it,
not just on the floor, but in your heart. There was
a sense of community.

We continued what we had started at the
opening ceremonies of M.A.S.T.E.R. Plan. At
every opportunity, as loud as we could, we
cheered our name. Everybody was watching us.
Freshman that had never met before, clustered
together, forming a community out of nothing.
Others were shocked at our presence. All week we
continued as that...building a community. That
week was the best week of my life.

Later that week, a young man came up and sat down with me while I was eating lunch. He simply said, "Thank you." "What do you mean," I asked? He replied, "Do you remember the other night when you got up and spoke to all us? You gave us all something to believe in. You made us believe in each other. You gave us family when we didn't have anything."

At that moment, I realized that I was doing had a purpose, and that it was good. All the planning, all of the preparation, the long hours cutting out door decorations, and bulletin boards was worth it. I knew that my job wasn't a job any more, it was a passion. A passion to help those who needed it, to teach and be taught, to listen to those who needed to talk, even at three o' clock in the morning. I realized that what I was doing was right because I was making a difference in the lives of people, who I now call my friends.

The campus was shaken by our enthusiasm, and when the upperclassmen returned from summer break, the new members of the North Hall Boys took over. They made friends with everyone, including returning students. They told everybody about their experiences. Then they challenged the others to have just as much enthusiasm. Our hall was off to a great start. Not only did I have the best semester that I have ever had in college, but our hall had it's best as well. We were winning awards left and right. We had men actively participating in RHA and Hall Government, and the men of North Hall were actually excited and proud to live in their hall... North Hall.

# Inspi*RA*tion for RAs

That semester I completed well over twenty programs and taught a Freshman Seminar class to follow up with Master Plan, in order to maintain the excitement that had been created during the first week. Two flag football teams were formed, and I captained both of them. I did my best to set the standard and be the leader of our RA community. I headed up socials; took charge in staff meetings; spoke up when a voice needed to be heard; and most of all, I listened with an open heart and an open mind.

My fire to be a great Resident Assistant never quit. I went on to end the semester winning a campus wide award for being the best Resident Assistant on campus. Academically, I finished with a 3.6 for the semester as well as being inducted into Phi Eta Sigma, a national college honor society. I have been a Resident Assistant for two semesters now and with time management skills I am able to maintain a high 3.6 cumulative Grade point average.

I have moved on from North Hall to another challenge. I currently work in the tallest residence hall in Kentucky. Pearce Ford Tower has twenty-seven floors and a staff of thirty-two members. My position as a Community Advisor (CA) now allows me to supervise and assist the Resident Assistants. This helps me teach them; I can pass my love for the position on to others, as well as role model positive attitudes and strong ideas. I will continue to spread my passion as long as I am here at Western Kentucky University. Constantly, I look for new challenges and adventures to further gain experience within the department, which I believe in very much. There is no paycheck that could ever buy what I have gained in experience and enjoyment while working as a Resident Assistant. There is no price that you can put on life long friendships, knowledge, and resource skills for everyday life. The Resident Assistant position is not a job or a career, but -a map for life and the opportunity to gain skills of experience. For me the Resident Assistant position is most importantly, a light unto those who we can help.

Brad Shuck – Community Advisor
Western Kentucky University
shuck2000@yahoo.com


*Make yourself necessary to someone.*
*-Ralph Waldo Emerson*

# Crisis by Candlelight

On April 20, 1999, the state of Colorado watched, horrified, as local television covered the school shooting at Columbine High School in Littleton, Colorado. As soon as the students and staff at Colorado State University found out about the tragedy, the university offered immediate support and response to the hundreds of Columbine graduates that were attending CSU. Many students also had a sibling, a friend, or former teacher at Columbine High School. The reactions of the students at Colorado State University were that of deep, profound grief and a quest for answers. With unprecedented speed and a sense of caring for the emotional impact on the campus, the university responded.

On the evening of the tragedy, the residence hall staff of Corbett Hall began a brainstorming session about how they could support the graduates of Columbine within their residence hall. Almost immediately, a solution became clear. The staff pulled resources together in order to organize a candlelight vigil for the Columbine students to share their grief, anger, and pain. What began as an effort to support the Columbine students in Corbett Hall became an effort to support the students, staff, and faculty of Colorado State University and then became an effort to support the needs of a grieving community.

Staff members canvassed the campus with flyers about the vigil, planned for the following evening in the courtyard of Corbett Hall. At the same time, an all-campus e-mail was sent out to notify staff and faculty on campus in order to help promote the event. The next morning, staff began working on the details of the vigil, which included getting candle donations, lighting, staging and sound equipment. The efforts also included working to provide counseling for grieving students and people to speak on behalf of the university and community.

That evening the staff and students of Corbett Hall were disappointed when a heavy rainstorm threatened the outdoor candlelight vigil. Knowing the importance of this event for a grieving campus, the staff and students of Corbett Hall moved the event into the dining center. Hundreds of students, staff, faculty, and community arrived to hear messages of grief and hope expressed by the local students and the mayor of Fort Collins.

The University's public relations office notified the media about the Corbett Hall vigil as well as other efforts being organized on behalf of Colorado State University faculty and staff. By late morning, the key players of the university discussed the events to respond with a unified effort. It was truly an incredible effort on the part of the university as the Registrar's Office and Housing and Food Services worked at identifying students that may be affected by the tragedy. The University Counseling Center issued an all-campus e-mail reminding staff, faculty and students to utilize the services provided by their office if they were having difficulty with their grieving.

As part of the vigil, the Associated Students of Colorado State University set up "several banners for people to sign to send a message of hope to the high school, its students, and staff"

At the same time, the Colorado State University Foundation agreed to collect money to assist the school, the victims and their families.

Reflecting back on that horrible day, it was so encouraging to see so many people come together as part of an effort this staff effort. It is nice to know when you have a community grieving, as many of our students were from Littleton, you also have the resources and energy to make a difference in peoples' lives.

Ray Gasser – Complex Coordinator
Colorado State University
rgasser@lamar.colostate.edu

Editor' Note: You can see more information at
**www.colostate.edu/Depts/PR/releases/news/csucares.html**

*We conquer by continuing.*
*George Matheson*


*Happiness is the by-product of an effort*
*to make someone else happy.*
*Greta Brooker Palmer*

# A Kindness Revisited

I was a second year RA at the University of New Mexico when I received a letter from a girl who had moved off my floor to return home because she was extraordinarily homesick. She wrote,

"Since I now have someone to compare your advising to, I can really say how much I appreciated you ... you always listened patiently and when you had to tell us to be quiet or to quit breaking rules, you did it in such a way that didn't bug us. In other words you did a fabulous job of being a RA and in retrospect I can say how much I appreciated it and how at home it made me feel. Thank you."

I have never received a letter like this, and while I hope that I someday receive another, I can say with heartfelt honesty that this first one is something that I will never forget and will treasure always. I was told when I took the RA position that it would be a growing and learning experience, and while it has had it's ups and downs, this simple act of kindness has made it all worthwhile.

Rebecca Casalino - Resident Advisor
University of New Mexico - PixieEize@aol.com

# Moments to Remember

As RAs, we hold a unique position where we rarely see the rewards for our hard work.  Seldom will we see our residents graduate, become their Sorority Presidents, or even be elected the Home-coming King for that matter.  As we journey through our college experience holding this posi-tion, I have found it is important to live for the moment, being sure to cherish the incredible experiences that face you every day.  I once told someone that while some people collect books, videos, photographs, or even animals, the most important thing I have found to collect is memo-ries.  When looking back on your RA experience now, or in the years to come, see if you can find these memories that have made such a difference in who you were, and who you became along the way.

**Remember Your First RA Training.**  Remember the countless hours of learning all of the duties and responsibilities that you would be expected to perform.  You were probably overwhelmed by the idea of learning all of your residents' names, let alone all the resources your campus had to offer.  As you frantically tried to finish all your door decorations and bulletin boards before the resi-dents arrived, I bet you wondered if you were cut out to be a student leader, or even a successful student on top of this job.

**Remember the First Time You Were Looked Upon as a Role Model.** You probably felt as though you didn't know what you were doing, yet a resident came up to you asking how you became the person they wanted to be. They may have joined the Hall Council because of you. They might have even become an RA on your staff a year later. It was at that moment when you realized that no one had it all worked out, and that those you looked up to were probably just as unsure of themselves and as disorganized as you were. But either way, you were going to make it!

**Remember the First Time You Had to Wipe Away Tears.** Although you probably thought you had been well trained and that you were ready to handle any situation, you were faced with the resident who came to you upset one night, and you weren't sure where to start. You stayed up with that resident all night listening to them, never once thinking about the mountain of homework you had, or the friends you were suppose to meet for coffee. And even though you thought you had been nothing more than a shoulder to cry on, you had became one of that residents' best friends.

**Remember the First Time You Had to Confront Someone.** You realized it was naive to think that every one of your residents would be a role model. As much as you feared doing it, you were faced with the dilemma of calling a resident on his or her actions. At the time, the fear was unimaginable yet you stayed your ground. You knew that your actions, although harsh, served a greater good. The second time you were placed in that situation, you were stronger because of it.

**Remember Late Night Pizza Parties.** As you learned the effective art of time management, you began to allow moments to "just happen" rather than trying to plan them weeks in advance. Every so often, you and a group of residents would chat around pizza until two in the morning. Who could forget nights of watching "Billy Madison" or "Tommy Boy" for the 18th time just to be with the group? Although much sleep was lost, you accepted it for these were the moments that defined college.

**Remember Feeling as Part of a Family.** You may not have grown up with brothers or sisters, or in a family as large as that of your hall staff. Having dinner in the cafeteria together, staying up all night philosophizing on life, or debating which was coolest toy when growing up; you began to realize that you had never been closer to a group a people as the fellow RAs and Hall Directors that you worked with. They had become closer than just friends, maybe even closer than family in some regards. As you look back, you take comfort in the fact that many of them are still your friends, and will continue to be.

**Remember Falling in Love.** Every day you were working, living, and playing with a group of people as close as your RA staff and it always led to strong friendships within the group.

Sometimes those friendships became deeper as time went by. Looking back, I'm sure may of you can think of one who almost seemed perfect in every way. They were more than just an infatuation because the two of you shared so much of your life together already. Whether they are now a broken heart or they're sitting right beside you, you cherish the RA position for having brought the two of you together.

**Remember the Failures, and Be Able to Laugh at Them.** Although you always tried to be successful in your position, there were undoubtedly the times where everything that could go wrong, did. Perhaps it was a Homecoming float that completely fell apart the night before the parade, or your program that attracted everyone you could hope for, except for your guest speaker. While at the time it seemed as though it was the end of the world, looking back the experience just make you giggle to yourself how silly it was to get worked up over something so small. The true meaning was not behind how everything turned out, but the fun it was doing it.

**And Finally, Remember the Achievement You Experienced as You Ended Your RA Experience.** As you finished your final months as an RA, you may have been quite taken back by the experience. The staff you were working with was far different than the people who welcomed you aboard. You had made numerous accomplishments, overcome challenges, and now, you were a leader to those just beginning their journey.

# Inspi*RA*tion for RAs

As you left your room, your floor, and your hall for the last time, you were upset by the fact that this was good-bye, but deep down, you acknowledged that you were excited too. For you would miss the experiences and people that had helped shape you through your college experience, you were now ready for the new destinations that lie ahead.

Jason Borges - Resident Assistant
Arizona State University
jason_sundevil@yahoo.com

*If you are interested in purchasing
"Moments to Remember"
in poster format, please contact:
The Collegiate EmPowerment Company
by calling toll free at 1-887-338-8246,
or email info@Collegiate-EmPowerment.com.

*"I loved being an RA. It brought me back to reality during my Ph.D. studies. Years later when I headed a university, I was much more student centered because of my RA experience. I'd love to do it again."*
- Donna Shalala, US Secretary of Health and Human Services and former Syracuse University RA.
(For a list of other famous RAs, see ResidentAssistant.com)

*We are the music makers.*
*We are the dreamers of dreams.*
*- Willy Wonka and the Chocolate Factory*

# About the Authors

**Dan Oltersdorf,** is the creator and founder of ResidentAssistant.com, the internationally acclaimed resource website for residence life. Dan worked in Residence Life at Colorado State University as an undergraduate in Human Development and Family Studies. He has a passion for students and believes "the RA position is one of the best opportunities to impact the lives of other students as well as enhance one's own personal growth. Dan continues to equip and empower students through his speaking, writing and online resources.

**Amy Connolly** is a native of the Chicago suburbs, where she held the R.A position for three years at Northern Illinois University. When she reflects on her R.A experience, Amy calls it "The hardest job I ever loved." Now, Amy continues to pursue interaction with college students in residence life through her motivational speaking and training. Amy's summary of the R.A position is simple - "Every R.A. is a friend, a confidant, a keeper of secrets, a teller of stories, and in the end, stronger for the experience."

**Tony D'Angelo** is recognized as the nation's leading authority of personal empowerment for today's college students. CNNfn has hailed him as "the personal development guru of his generation" and SPIN Magazine has compared him with the likes of motivational superstar, Anthony Robbins. As creator of EmPower X! and The Collegiate EmPowerment Company, Tony has impacted the lives of over 800,000 college students from over 800 colleges throughout North America with his nationally acclaimed **What College Forgets To Teach You**® Seminar Series.

*If You'd Like To Bring Dan, Amy, Tony*
*Or An EmPower X! Coach To Speak*
*At Your Campus, Please Contact:*
**The Collegiate EmPowerment Company, Inc.**
**Call Toll Free: 1-877-EDUTAIN (338-8246)**
**Email: Info@Collegiate-EmPowerment.com**

# More Inspi*RA*tion!

## *Would You Like To See*
## *YOUR Story In A Future RA Book?*

All of the stories and poems that you have read in this book were submitted by readers like you who are RA's and Residence Life Professionals in the front lines. We would love to have you contribute a story, poem, quote or cartoon to future books for RA's. Future RA books include:

**InspiRAtion for RA's Vol. II:**
*More Inspiring Stories for RA's by RA's*
**ProgRAmming for RA's:**
*101 Kick-Ass Programming Ideas for RA's by RA's*
**PrepaRAtion for RA's:**
*A training and reference guide*

Feel free to send us stories you write yourself or even ones that you clip out of your campus newspaper. It could also be a favorite poem, quotation, cartoon, idea, suggestion you have seen that speaks to your RA experience. Just make sure to send us as much information about you and the source of your submission. Please send your submissions to:

**The Collegiate EmPowerment Company, Inc.**
**Submission Department: InspiRAtion For RA's**
**PO Box 702, Lambertville, New Jersey 08530**
**Fax: 609-397-0833**
**Email: RAbooks@Collegiate-EmPowerment.com**

If accepted & approved, your submission will be published in a future edition and will touch the lives of thousands of RAs across the country!
Of course you'll get a free book too!

**Editor's note: Hillary Clinton, who was an RA at Wellesly College, still has not sent in a story submission. We're still waiting, Hillary!**

# Giving back to you

We feel strongly about giving back to everyone who has made this book possible. The hard work and dedication that each of these stories represent is what makes a difference in the lives of millions of on-campus residents every year. With this in mind, we have chosen three benefactors to receive proceeds from the sales of **InspiRAtion for RAs:**

**The Association of College And University Housing Officers International (ACUHO-I)** - ACUHO-I is the nation's largest association serving Housing & Residence Life Officers in Higher Education. ACUHO-I was founded in 1951 in response to the unprecedented rise in college enrollment after World War II and the subsequent concerns of housing and feeding this growing student population. Today the association boasts an membership of over 5,800 individuals from over 900 colleges and universities serving 1.8 million students worldwide. www.acuho.ohio-state.edu

**National Association of College and University Residence Halls (NACURH)** - NACURH's purpose is to design and facilitate programs and informational services to promote the educational goals of the residence hall students. NACURH does this through regional and national conferences, program development, leadership training and communication and information exchange through a communication network between all colleges and universities. - www.nacurh.com

**Daughter, Friend, Co-worker, Student, Hero and Inspiration**
On January 19, 2000 at Seton Hall University, a fire that resulted in 3 fatalities started. In this horrible tragedy, a spirit rose above the ashes to touch us all. Dana Christmas is just like you, an RA who has compassion for her residents. Dana woke and pounded on the doors of her residents, taking each one outside. Dana returned to her floor several times. On her fourth entry, Dana did not return. When she was rescued, over 60% of her body was burned. At the time of this writing, Dana is still in critical condition. We are giving a portion of the proceeds of this book to help with her medical bills. We are also asking you to lend a hand to a fallen RA whose spirit, commitment and action serves as an inspiration to us all. To make a donation on Dana's behalf please forward it to: The Dana Christmas InspiRAtion Fund, c/o The Collegiate EmPowerment Company, PO Box 702, Lambertville, NJ 08530 - (Please make checks payable to The Dana Christmas InspiRAtion Fund) Thank you for your generosity!

# ResidentAssistant.com
## "The Rx for RAs"

ResidentAssistant.com is the leading online resource for residence hall staff members. Founded in December of 1998 by Dan Oltersdorf, the site consists of hundreds of pages of resources, including:

- **Programming ideas in different categories**
- **Pre-made bulletin boards for you to print out**
- **Advice articles on everything from roommates to suicide**
- **Humorous stories from RAs**
- **Ask the Experts - Submit your questions to professionals**
- **Discussion forums**
- **Free web-based email**
- **Free monthly email newsletter**
- **RA list-serve**
- **Residence life related books and products**
- **Hundreds of links to other resources, on and off the web**

The resources and advice on this site are submitted by you, the professionals and student staff who live and work on the front lines. The continued growth of this site is a great testament to the dedication all of you have to serving students, and will continue to grow only with your help. Be sure to continue submitting your successful programs and your advice articles. If you are a professional, and you would like to write advice articles and/or serve on our panel of experts, answering questions from RAs all over the world, please email info@residentassistant.com.

Be sure to visit ResidentAssistant.com on a regular basis to find out what is new on the site. We hope it proves to be a great resource that helps you to better serve your residents.

**www.ResidentAssistant.com**

# The Collegiate EmPowerment Company, Inc.

*The Leader In EmPowerment Education For Today's College Students*[TM]

The Collegiate EmPowerment Company is a nationally recognized educational firm dedicated to coaching college students who are looking to create a balanced and meaningful life. Sadly enough most college students go to college and get a degree, but not an education. We are dedicated to serving Student Affairs Professionals and Student Leaders like you by Helping You Take Higher Education Deeper. We achieve this goal through our What College Forgets To Teach You® Seminar Series & our EmPower X! Instructional Team. The seminar series is the most comprehensive personal development curriculum ever designed for young adults aged 18-28. With over 30 dynamic and edutaining seminars we Help Today's College Students Get An Education While They Earn Their Degree.

### Here's a sampling of the
### What College Forgets To Teach You® Seminars:

*You Can't Lead Others Until You First Lead Yourself*
**What College Forgets To Teach You About Personal Leadership**

*If You Think You Can Or You Think You Can't, Either Way You're Right*
**What College Forgets To Teach You About Personal Beliefs**
**(The Karate Board Breakthrough)**

*Why Most Student Organizations Don't Work & What To Do About It*
**What College Forgets To Teach You About Being A Student Leader**

*The Seven Jedi Mind Tricks Every RA Needs To Know*
**What College Forgets To Teach You About Being A Resident Assistant**

*It's Not Just a Job, It's a Lifestyle*
**What College Forgets To Teach You (Freshman Orientation)**

*Men Are Like Microwaves & Women Are Like Crockpots*
**What College Forgets To Teach You About Relationships**

*How to maximize your BUZZ!*
**What College Forgets To Teach You About Alcohol**

- All of our seminars are fun, high-energy, interactive, multimedia experiences that relate to college students.

- All of our seminars synergize with each other which offers long-term results and residual impact.

- We offer multiple visits to your campus each semester which allows students to benefit exponentially.

- All of our seminars are developed by young adults for young adults.

- All of our instructors are under the age of 30.

- Everything we do is backed by a 100% money back guarantee.

- If you and your students don't like it, you don't pay for it.

To Learn How To Bring A Collegiate EmPowerment Coach To Your Campus or To Request A Collegiate EmPowerment Company Information Kit Please Call Toll Free: 1-877-EDUTAIN (338-8246) or visit us at www.Collegiate-EmPowerment.com

# Ordering Information

## Order InspiRAtion for RA's By The Case & Save Big!

The Perfect Gift For Your RAs! Are you looking for a great way to say- thank you, good luck, welcome aboard or job well done to your Residence Life Team? Why not order this book direct and save money!

As a Residence Life Professional you're entitled to these exclusive bulk order discounts:

### RATE SCHEDULE:

| Case Size | # of BOOKS | Approx. Discount | Price Per Copy | Bulk Rate Discount | YOU SAVE | S&H | TOTAL PRICE |
|---|---|---|---|---|---|---|---|
| ½ | 25 | 15% | $12.70 | $317.50 | $56.25 | $10 | $327.50 |
| 1 | 50 | 20% | $12.00 | $600.00 | $147.50 | $20 | $620.50 |
| 1 ½ | 75 | 25% | $11.25 | $843.75 | $277.50 | $25 | $868.75 |
| 2 | 100 | 30% | $10.50 | $1050.00 | $445.00 | $40 | $1090.00 |
| 3 | 150 | 35% | $9.75 | $1462.50 | $780.00 | $50 | $1512.50 |
| 4 | 200 | 40% | $9.00 | $1800.00 | $1190.00 | $60 | $1860.00 |

*Please note this special discount offer is only offered on ½ case and full case orders. Quantity ordered must be either 25, 50, 75, 100, 150 or 200. Sorry no exceptions.*
*We accept credit cards, checks, money orders and purchase orders*

To Order or For More Information, Please Contact:
The Collegiate EmPowerment Company, Inc.
Toll Free: 1-877-EDUTAIN (338-8246)
Email: Info@Collegiate-EmPowerment.com
www.Collegiate-EmPowerment.com
*Thank You For You Interest!*
*We Look Forward To Serving You!*